Department of Health

CHILD ABUSE

A Study of Inquiry Reports
1980–1989

London: HMSO

First published 1991

ISBN 0 11 321391 3

introduction

1. This Report on Child Abuse Inquiries 1980–89 is a companion volume to the publication in 1982 which reviewed the lessons of child abuse inquiries from 1973–1981. It covered 18 reports. Inquiries continued to be held during the 80s and this study reviews 19 further inquiry reports.

2. The interdisciplinary team at the Department of Health which advises Ministers on policy in relation to the prevention and treatment of child abuse produced the first volume. The team remains in being albeit with a complete change of membership. It was decided, however, to adopt a different procedure for the production of a second volume and an outside expert with experience of child abuse policy was asked to read all 19 reports and record his cumulative impressions. Phillip Noyes, Head of Public Policy at the National Society for the Prevention of Cruelty to Children, kindly agreed to do this and this volume is his response.

3. An interesting feature of inquiries is that there is no standard format. Issues received different emphasis in the reports, some are not covered at all and some are only covered in a small number. For instance, there is very little on race and gender, issues which are receiving much more attention in the 1990s. What was remarkable in the first decade of inquiries was the coherence of the findings. In the 1980s a more complicated picture emerges. The messages from the last decade of reports may seem depressing but it is understandable where difficult decisions concerning human relationships are being made by professional staff from a number of agencies that tragedies will from time to time occur. For this reason continual alertness to the lessons of the past is an essential element of a well run child protection service.

4. The mid 1980s saw an increase in the reporting of child abuse. It is not known whether or not the actual incidence of abuse has increased. Public awareness of child abuse increased and critical in this was the emergence of child sexual abuse as a problem which shocked, but possibly not surprised, the public. Among other things the emergence of child sexual abuse has led to increased recognition of power and gender as factors inherent in the abuse of children. Associated with this has been increased awareness of the rights and needs of children. 'The child is a person and not an object of concern'.

5. The importance of some of the findings and recommendations of the Reports required immediate action and policy has not stood still during the last decade. The Department of Health has ensured that many of the messages have been the subject of new policy advice and guidance through Working Together 1988 and the Children Act 1989. Research has been commissioned to explore questions raised by the Reports and Departmental training initiatives have focused on the needs of key participants in the child protection process.

6. The proper balance of judgement between respecting family privacy and intervention to protect a child must always be difficult to achieve. Most of the reports describe cases which require professionals to work with families who are either resistant and hostile to their intervention and hence are frightening or superficially

plausible and the so-called 'rule of optimism' may prevail. Apart from the constant reminder of the need to see the child at appropriate intervals, good supervision of the professional worker and mutual support of colleagues of other professions are the best response. Although no system, however good, will remove the conflicts and difficulties with which workers have to deal.

7.   Progress in establishing good interagency working has been made during the 80s. The publication of Working Together – in 1988 with the reconstitution of ARCs as Area Child Protection Committees (ACPCs) gave an opportunity to take stock. The process of reviewing procedures and establishing ACPCs on a sound footing is not yet completed everywhere. Moreover the Children Act 1989 with inter alia improved court orders for handling child protection will be implemented in October 1991 and Working Together will be revised to take account of the changes. This volume is intended as a contribution to this process.

8.   This document on a decade of Inquiry Reports takes a wide ranging look at the complexity of issues which have emerged. We hope that this publication will be used to stimulate debate about issues in practice and management. For example, the sections on supervision could be used by those establishing local policies to consider content, purpose and methods of supervision in child protection work. Similarly, the sections on case conferences could be used to inform local review of procedures. We see this as a useful source of reference to trainers, policy advisers, middle managers and social work academics in their difficult task of developing and improving child protection services.

REFERENCES

'A'   Mr and Mrs 'A' (private report). 1989

DA   Doreen Aston. 1989

JB   Jasmine Beckford. 1985

RC   Reuben Carthy. 1985

CLV   Cleveland inquiry. 1988

JC   Jason Caesar. 1982

KC   Kimberley Carlile. 1987

RF   Richard Fraser. 1982

LGC   Lucy Gates (Chairman's report). 1982

LGP   Lucy Gates (Panel's report). 1982

CH   Claire Haddon. 1980

EJH   Emma Jane Hughes. 1981

TH   Tyra Henry. 1987

LJ   Liam Johnson. 1989

HK   Heidi Koseda. 1986

KMcG   Karl McGoldrick. 1989

CP   Christopher Pinder. 1981

JP   Jason Plischkowsky. 1988

CS   Charlene Salt. 1986

SW   Shirley Woodcock (Summary report). 1984

contents

APPENDICES

agency context

Child protection work requires statutory and voluntary agencies to work together with parents and children. It requires individuals employed by statutory and voluntary agencies to work together. In this section what the reports have to say about agency functions is considered. The reports continue to demonstrate, as they did during the 1970s, that problems can arise where there is lack of clarity about the different contributions of the various agencies and individuals involved.

At the heart of the inquiry of the 80s has been a developing debate about the role of statutory agencies intervening in the family life, in particular, the role of the local authority social worker. At the same time inquiries have brick by brick strengthened the area review committee, now area child protection committee, rule framework. Professionals working in the field of child protection are regulated not by one set of rules, but two. Inter-agency working is not easy and is not self evidently useful. It needs strategic planning and active efforts. Differences of approach between agencies are not easy to deal with. What is needed in common, is high priority to child protection and a commitment to action.

Reports address the standards of their own judgements and address, directly and indirectly, who is to blame for the child death, and the preceding miseries. Inquiries repeatedly identify 'some unacceptably low professional standards, incidence of poor line management, poor communication among social workers however professional, specific breaches of departmental policies, poor recording and the clouding of professional judgement'. ('A' 3) Yet reports do not have recourse to a standard of practice against which to judge.

Inquiries note the political instability that prevails in local government with its inevitable effects on staff. They emphasise the strain on individuals, 'the high levels of anxiety involved in this work of the relentless pressure, of the tensions and the feelings of guilt which ran the professional lives of those who worked to protect children for whom their agency is responsible'. ('A' 2) Yet the nature of child protection work, and the pressure of structures are not brought together to describe the impact of the work on practitioners.

The inquiries describe the impact of organisational change on services in a way that might serve as a lesson for the 90s as Community Care, NHS reorganisation, and implementation of the Children Act take place.

1.1 LOCAL AUTHORITY SOCIAL SERVICES DEPARTMENT

Legal duties for child, parents, community

The 1933 and 1969 Children and Young Persons Acts contain the main provisions relating to the care and protection of children who are being abused, or are at risk of abuse. Child care law has now been substantially overhauled with the passing of the Children Act 1989. The inquiries of the 80s comment extensively on local authority responsibilities, and how they are discharged.

The complexity of the social work role and task

Double standards operate in the field of child protection. Many of the inquiries note the difficulties in, and complexities of, social work tasks. The final submission to the Cleveland inquiry of the Social Services Department pointed out 'the Social Services, of course, always have a thankless task. If they are overcautious and take children away from their families they are pilloried for doing so. If they do not take such action and do not take the child away from the family and something terrible happens to the child, then likewise they are pilloried'. (CLV 85) At the same time inquiries recognise there is no way in which social services departments can effectively monitor a situation so as to prevent the child dying in consequences or incidents of violence and injuries, except by removing that child from home altogether. (LJ 3.94)

The Kimberley Carlile inquiry considered that social workers are entitled to some special treatment when it comes to public accountability. 'As a class of public servants they are patronised by professionals in the law and in medicine; they are vilified by the popular press; they are disliked by sections of the public who misunderstand, or are ignorant of what social work is about; their failures are consistently highlighted . . . . . . Until the public is prepared to accord social workers the status granted to others who have to perform difficult tasks for public benefit, some redress of public opprobrium is not out of place.' (KC 7)

Social workers are . . . . . . employed to provide help, assistance, support and sympathy for their clients, and to promote and make possible change in even the most inevident people. (JB 202) Such a relationship involves attaining co-operation from the child or parent so that something positive can be achieved. (CH 3.4.2 also CLV 27)

However, the social work role, as is explored in particular in the Beckford inquiry, is more than this. 'Social workers are also required by society to carry out certain duties and exercise powers, and these duties and powers are laid down in acts of parliament. These may require the social workers to implement decisions to go against the wishes of the client, and to exercise control if, in their professional judgement, the life and well being of a client – who may often be a child – is at risk. This dual mandate . . . . . . imposes responsibilities for both social care and social control.' (JB 202)

The Beckford inquiry contentiously notes that 'high risk' 'is not susceptible of definition', and suggests that 'rather than indulge in a massive reinvestment of resources, which at the optimum can minimise marginally the risk of injury, fatal or serious, to the child at home . . . . . . society should sanction in high risk cases the removal from home of such children for appreciable time . . . . . . It is on those children who are at risk – but where the risk is problematical – that Social Services should concentrate their efforts'. (JB 288–289)

A further complication is noted by the Doreen Aston inquiry. 'There is a popular feeling commonly expressed that children must be protected from danger. The simple fact is that under legislation existing in 1986 and 1987 children were not offered protection from danger. Social pressures have sometimes caused child welfare agencies to act as if they had those powers, but when they are exercised the same social pressures will say that the child should be protected from the danger of removal from parents.' (DA 7.32)

Multiple roles

One problem is the perception of the purpose of social work. The chair of the Lucy Gates Chairman's report noted that in his view child care is specialist work and requires suitably trained field worker, yet there is a lack of clarity about training for what purpose. The inquiry notes social workers and health visitors attempt to understand the client and try to motivate change, and questions whether they were qualified to undertake what they appeared to be attempting 'this was work for a psychiatrist or a psychologist'. (LGC 39.20) The Panel Report puts training into a wider context.

There is a need for finely tuned decision making. The Kimberley Carlile inquiry judges the quality of social work performed by social workers responding to an anonymous call. 'It is never enough simply to comply with the letter of the state of procedures . . . . . . There is always an overriding professional duty to exercise skill, judgement and care.' (KC 96)

'Can a social worker fulfil a policing role, firmly and efficiently, if he has also to gain the family's confidence, and to convey the personal warmth and the genuineness necessary for him to provide the support which will enable them to become better parents? . . . . . .

The duality of approach is by no means impossible to achieve, providing that the worker is clear about the nature of the job. It is essential that the worker recognises that he owes allegiance to both the agency (and society) which requires him to be a child protector, and at the same time to the parent on whose trust he can build a relationship.' (JB 14–15)

The inquiry notes that 'Authority' is not a dirty word. Indeed, it must be brought officially from behind the arras of social work training onto the public stage, not just of child care law but also into the practice of all social workers. We regard this as an essential ingredient in any work designed to protect abused children'. (JB 295)

Parental rights and responsibilities

Another dimension to the dilemma is added by a number of inquiries, namely 'the rights of parents which appear to take precedence over the rights of children. There is confusion over what the rights of children are. There is currently strong pressure on professional workers as to keep children with their parents at almost any cost.' (LGP 6.17)

The Kimberley Carlile inquiry notes that 'in many social workers there lurks a lack of confidence about their duty to insist on seeing a child in their parents' home, when access to that child is being determinedly refused. This lack of confidence stems, partly, we think, from an uncertainty about the nature and the extent of powers granted to social workers in pursuance of their investigative duties in relation to child abuse . . . . . . The lack of confidence also in part, springs from a healthy respect for parental rights. But when it is the safety of a child in its parents' home, parental rights must yield to child protection'. (KC 101–102)

'Policing' parents

The Tyra Henry inquiry also addresses 'policing'. It understands and accepts ethical and practical objections to 'social workers acting as intelligence gathering agents' . . . . . . 'It is one thing for a neighbour to report seeing Claudette Henry and Andrew Neil in the street together; it is another for a social worker to visit the neighbour in search of such information.' Openness about role can lay the basis for more effective 'intelligence gathering', 'if, for instance, Andrew Neil had been seen or spoken to about Tyra at the start, as proper procedure and practice required, there would have been little if any problem of openly visiting him and his family later on in order to monitor the situation'. (TH 7.16)

Inquiry reports do not attempt to specify an optimum frequency of visiting. They concentrate on relating frequency of visiting to the needs of the case, and some note that quality rather than quantity of visiting is what is important, and repeatedly call for the Boarding Out Regulations to be enforced.

When to remove the child?

The removal of the child from the care of the parents is an awesome responsibility. 'Social workers have a duty in law to ensure the protection of children where they have cause to believe that there is a high risk of further immediate abuse. If that risk cannot be modified by the withdrawal from the home of the person whose behaviour is believed to pose a risk to the child; or the non abusing parent cannot be relied upon to protect the child; and in the absence of the parents agreement to the child admission to the hospital, an application to magistrates for a place of safety order may be inevitable'. (CLV 13.4) Thus are established criteria for this onerous decision.

The inquiry goes on to note that the experiences of children in the care of the local authority are significantly fashioned by the manner in which they were initially received into care. The social worker thus needs to make the plans in relation to their personal needs, and it is difficult to achieve these arrangements when children are received into care in an emergency or dramatic manner. 'These considerations should give importance to social workers efforts to secure the protection of the child by achieving an agreement with the parent or care giver. They do not, however, constitute a reason for leaving the child in a situation where he is at higher risk of further abuse or violence.' (CLV 13.6)

'Society, rightly in our opinion, is not prepared to tolerate too heavy handed disruptions to family life, and expects careful judgement to be exercised in deciding on the appropriate action to be taken with any particular case. This more flexible approach offers some security to families. But, given that human judgement is fallible, society must tolerate occasional failure.' (KC 136)

Prevention or protection?

The law places the main responsibility for preventative work and for initiating action to protect children on the Social Services Department. The NSPCC also has power to intervene and initiate action although normally after consultation with Social Services Departments. The police, who have powers to intervene, will not usually act before consulting the Social Services. Education departments possess some powers but are required to consult with Social Services. (LGC 30.1) 'The leit-motif of modern child care law is preventive action. To that end, a general duty is imposed on a local authority to provide support for a child and his family and thereby avoid the child being received or taken into care by the local authority . . . . . . The local authority, in exercising its duty has a complete discretion . . . . . . The decision on any child must depend entirely on the different circumstances of each child being individually considered by the local authority.' (JB 17)

Responsibilities to children in care

Local authorities and its employees are subject to a wide range of specified statutory duties in respect of children taken into care; a local authority is both accountable to its electorate and liable in law for breach in its statutory duty. The Tyra Henry inquiry analyses legal constraints on the local authority in its consideration of whether to exercise statutory powers for the protection of Tyra Henry after her birth. The choice of measures to be taken for the child was a matter of its discretion. All discretionary decisions made must be consciously based on all available and relevant data. (TH 6.2) The legal and practical implications of the care order in this specific context of this case arise morally from the simple fact that the (care) order makes the local authority answerable for the care of the child. 'The reason why Tyra was able to slip out of the care, control and protection of the local authority, of her grandmother and finally her mother, was, in a word, that sight was lost of whose child she was . . . . . . The overriding responsibility of Lambeth as Tyra's legal parent became lost in the tangle of the administrative frustration and professional misjudgment that we have traced.' (TH 13.1) 'It seems to have escaped notice that any failure that effected Tyra's well being was both legally and morally Lambeth's failure, even if it were a simple omission to have Tyra immunised.' (TH 3.37)

The Beckford inquiry goes further in its description of the local authority responsibilities to children in its care. 'Parental rights and duties do not transfer to local authority. They are in suspended animation during the currency of the care order. We have concluded that the nature of the local authority's responsibility for a child in care, who is received into care voluntarily or taken in compulsorily, is one of trust . . . . . . The local authority is bound by the trust reposed in it by society, through the agency of the juvenile court, to safeguard and promote the interests of the child in its care. To do so, it may have to take steps that go beyond mere sound parenting . . . . . . we would want the law to state that a child in care is a child in trust.' (JB 19–21) In its conclusion the inquiry notes that the making of a care order itself invests Social Services with pervasive preventive powers.

In consideration of all the circumstances once the child is in care, and in the view of the Tyra Henry inquiry before application is made (TH 8.13) local authorities must consider available resources to service the cause of action that is decided upon.

Some reports note the responsibilities for the continuing care of children. In view of the number of young parents of children in these inquiries who are still in care at the time of their children's birth, or having shortly left care this is an important point. (RF 7. CH 1)

Advising and assisting the local authority

Social Services do not work in a vacuum. They depend on other specialist services for suggestions and advice. (LGC 76.3) The Lucy Gates Panel inquiry stated that 'health professionals have a duty to assist Social Services colleagues in the health care and management of children'. The inquiries provide examples of agencies not advising and assisting the local authority. Perhaps most bluntly: 'we are satisfied that if the existence of the scarring across Reuben Carthy's back together with the admission of the mother that she had caused the scarring had been referred to the Social Services Department (by the GP) (protective) action would have been taken . . . . . . we are satisfied that if the presenting circumstances had been referred to the Social Services on 21st January 1985 Reuben Carthy would not have died on the 4th February 1985'. (RC 134)

Proposals are made throughout the inquiries to formalise the process of assisting and advising, for example through automatic notification of Social Services when a clinical appointment for a child in care or at risk is not kept. (TH 10.4 also LJ 2.0.1) The inquiry into Mr and Mrs 'A' identified problems involving relationships between education and health and within the health profession itself. 'A number of more general issues emerged from this element of our inquiry, mostly the role of the 'non-social services' agencies in child protection (does their duty extend beyond notifying the Social Services Department of their concern? If notification is ignored, what should they properly do?).' ('A' 12)

The Beckford inquiry notes that section 22 (1) National Health Service Act 1977 already imposes a duty on health authorities and local authorities to co-operate in the discharge of the respective functions. 'We think there are powerful reasons why their duties should be made more specific, to include the duty to consult and a duty to assist by advice and the supply of information in the process of the management of the child abuse system . . . . . . Historically all the emphasis has been placed on involving all the other agencies and identifying child abuse, rather than in the management of the child abuse system in all its stages. The statutory duty should spell out the fact that the duties involved are reciprocal . . . . . . A statutory definition of the duty to consult and a correlative duty to advise may improve the perception of other agencies as to their role, with a correspondent improvement in the confidence in the health visitor herself.' (JB 144) The Kimberley Carlile inquiry takes this further by recommending a specific duty on the health authority to promote the welfare of the children.

Relationship of the Social Services Department to the public

Passing information
The local community can be of assistance to the main agencies to help children at risk and their families. (RF 148) The Kimberley Carlile inquiry asks how a member of the public is to judge the degree of risk? Probably the most helpful advice that could be offered the members of the public is to tell them to trust their instincts and back their own judgement. Such action, even if it is subsequently proved to have been mistaken or unnecessary, is justifiable if based on concern for a child. Inaction, and a child suffering unnecessarily as a result, cannot be justified . . . . . . (Child Protection Agencies) 'must cultivate an attitude which welcomes contact from the public . . . Organisations concerned about the adequacy of the resources at their disposal will be worried about generating demand for their services, but this should not be translated into wanting to turn off the referrals unless we are prepared to remain ignorant generally of the level of demand, and ignorant specifically of the needs of an individual child. The agencies receiving referral from the public should be clear how to respond . . . . . . All agencies must have policy to take such referrals seriously and must make certain that they are followed up to the point that a decision can be made concerning the welfare of the child referred'. (KC 200–201)

The Heidi Koseda report notes 'concerns felt by members of the public should be expressed, even if they turn out to be without substance, and equally important that they should be listened to with the utmost care by the professional staff'. The Authority must respond. (HK 3)

The Lucy Gates Panel report also notes the assistance that neighbours might be both in helping the parents, and by taking direct action to protect children. 'We consider that publicity should be given to the power of any citizen to make application to a magistrate for the temporary removal of a child to a place of safety.' (LGP) The Lucy Gates Chairman's report suggests the publicity could usefully urge the public never to hesitate to notify the Social Services,

NSPCC or the Police when they know that children are left unattended.

Perhaps most emphatic of all is the need for parents and children themselves to be prepared to contact the relevant authority. The Liam Johnson inquiry considers why the father's cohabitee did not disclose the risk to the children after she left the father. It goes on to identify a number of factors. 'Most importantly, however, we do not think that it ever occurred to her to do so.' (LJ 4.16–4.18)

Other workers and services

The inquiry reports note the need for the local authority to liaise with a range of statutory and voluntary bodies. Their roles, and the roles of other workers within the Social Services Department must be appreciated.

The important role for home care and day care staff, nurseries and pre-school provision is noted in a number of inquiries. The demands of an added 'policing' dimension to home care duties are noted, and good communication with social workers and adequate training called for. (LGC 24.9, 15.2, 61.3) The day nursery can provide baseline information about a child's development. (SW 1.67) The nursery staff are able to keep detailed notes on the child's progress as well as the general situation of the family. Moreover day nursery staff can be the first in line in identifying child abuse. (RF 16) However, whilst day care has a valuable role to play the views of nursery staff are not always taken as sufficiently seriously as they might be (CS 13, for example). Day nurseries have a more general preventative role. The role of day nurseries in preventing in family break up and the need for local authority care, and the role in prevention of child abuse was emphasised in a report from the Director of Social Services to the Reuben Carthy inquiry. (RC 94) The Lucy Gates Panel inquiry noted 'the important contribution of the pre-school playgroup movement and the need for continuing support from national and local governments'. (LGP 5.23)

The Local Authority Housing Department

Some reports pay attention to the need for effective working relationships between Social Services Departments and Housing Department. Housing Departments can provide important information and a number of inquiries note the need to make a check with the Housing Department before an initial case conference to see if they have relevant information and should attend (for example JC 3.4.24). The Gates case demonstrated the need for joint planning and close co-operation and decision making between the Social Services Department and the Housing Department. (LGC 46.4)

The Tyra Henry inquiry discusses the role of Social Services and Housing Departments in the circumstances of a child being in the care of the local authority. It is the local authority corporately which bears the responsibility for providing the accommodation and maintenance needed to protect a child in its care. (TH 6.9) The report considered it scandalous that Lambeth was unable to provide one of its own dwellings to enable Beatrice Henry to do the council's own job of keeping Tyra well and safe. 'We have made it clear earlier in this report our grave concern that Tyra's legal care was undertaken by the council without first making adequate provision to fulfil the task. It is equally a matter of the utmost seriousness even within the overstretched and attenuated resources available to the council the means which have existed to make such provision were frustrated by sheer administrative inefficiency when the task was attempted.' (TH 8.1.3) The inquiry recommends a method of housing allocation which enables routine cases to be routinely and equitably dealt with, but which ensures that special cases are singled out and handled at a higher level as necessary to get them resolved. (TH 8.17)

1.2 NSPCC

Powers

The NSPCC has the power to bring care proceedings in its own right. The Beckford inquiry notes this is a unique role for a voluntary organisation. In practice 'the Society's main function is to receive information, evaluate it and take appropriate action. In only a small proportion of its cases the Society takes care proceedings; . . . It frequently applies for place of safety orders'. (JB 175) The Lucy Gates Chairman report quotes NSPCC procedures 'The Society's first duty must be to respond to complaints and referrals where children are (or are likely to be) assaulted, or ill treated or neglected by person having custody, charge or care of them, and this must take priority over all other work. In any situation the Society's first concern must be for the immediate safety of children and for action directed to this end'. (LGC 29.3)

Being accessible

The Heidi Koseda inquiry considers the question of the desirability of the continuance with dual system of service (by Social Service and the NSPCC), which had been discussed fully in the report into the death of Marie Colwell some years previously. It states 'whether or not the NSPCC continues to provide an *investigation and child protection* service in the Borough, we think that its role as a recipient of referrals from the public is important and should be maintained. The referrer in this case told us that as a Council tenant, she would have been apprehensive in approaching her local Social Services Department, whereas the NSPCC seem to afford a degree of anonymity, and was the source to which she naturally turned. It is abundantly clear that neighbours are generally those with the key information and that every possible channel of communication of their concern should be kept open'. (HK 2.33 original underlining)

Both the Beckford inquiry and Lucy Gates reports note the value of NSPCC attendance at case conferences. The Jason Caesar inquiry also notes the value of this but recognises that staffing levels might mean that NSPCC could not attend many case conferences.

Independence of view

The Lucy Gates inquiry considers at some length the role of the NSPCC in relation to decision making about care proceedings. 'We believe that the NSPCC should challenge the approach of a Social Services Department in particular cases, if it is the view of the Society that care proceedings are the wisest course.' (LGP 3.5.5) The Chairman's Report also expresses this view 'it may be that since the coming into force of the Children And Young Persons Act 1969, which requires them to consult with the Social Services, (the NSPCC) have felt less free to act independently than hitherto. They should not feel that. The child's safety may depend upon their independent judgement and action'. (LGC)

1.3 HEALTH AUTHORITY

Health authorities provide maternity and community health services for children, including domiciliary health visiting and child health centres. There is a statutory requirement for health and local authorities to co-operate. The health services are responsible for the surveillance of all children at key ages and for preventive and health promotional activities. These services are important in relation to the detection of child abuse (LGP 5.37) and to the protection of children generally.

In some areas, high level of social need, poor housing conditions, a high proportion of lone parents, highly mobile population often not well supported by family networks, and poverty, makes the delivery of effective health care, a complicated and hard task for those planning, managing and delivering services. (DA 4.12)

The inquires comment extensively on the need for effective communication both within all parts of the health service and with other agencies.

Medical and social assessment

Reports emphasise the importance of properly documented medical assessments against which progress can be monitored. The Kimberley Carlile and the Jasmine Beckford inquiries emphasise that information gathered at developmental assessments should be considered in the light of previous information about the child. The Doreen Aston inquiry emphasises the importance of medical assessments in a child protection context. 'Doreen was seen by the community medical officer as one of about 15–20 children she examined that morning. For the doctor, Doreen's check did not stand out from the rest that morning. She was not aware of the case conference had regarded this check as of considerable importance.' (DA 2.147)

The Beckford report criticises doctors seeing their functions in strictly medical terms instead of utilising their medical skills in the wider context of social policy and practice. It notes barriers in the training of physicians which emphasises 'being in charge, taking decisions, hearing and even listening to other professional views, but still taking decisions based upon their own medical judgement'. (JB 82; also CLV 8.8.46, 8.9.26; JC 3.4.31)

A number of reports point out the influence doctors assessments can have: 'if he tells them that their fears of child abuse are not justified they may become quiescent when they should be inquisitive. On the other hand, field workers misunderstand that very often a doctor's assessment of the situation depends on what he himself is told'. (LGC 55.2)

The Charlene Salt report notes the importance of feedback from assessments and recommends that whenever a child on the register is seen for such assessment, the health visitor involved should be present, or there should be a written report outlining the position and informing the doctor of anxieties the health visitor has. (CS 18)

Thus medical assessments must clearly be put into context. Direct communication with the health visitor before and after assessment are of prime importance. The limitations of an episodic medical assessment must be recognised.

Community services

The role of the health visitor
The health visitor figures in all cases. The Doreen Aston inquiry considers the role of the health visitor in detail. It quotes the National Health Service Regulations 1972 which define the health visitor as 'the person employed by a local authority to visit people in their homes or elsewhere for the purpose of giving advice to the care of young children, the person suffering from illness and expectant or nursing mothers, and as to the measures necessary to prevent the

spread of infection, and includes the person so employed by a voluntary organisation within a local health authority'. (DA 4.18) The individual health visitor is not given statutory powers of duties.

The nature or essence of health visiting lies, in the view of the Health Visitors Association quoted by the inquiry, in its primarily pro-active role, in which health visitors actively search for health needs rather than waiting for them to be uncovered by others. This search leads in its turn to an active initiation of change in attitudes, behaviours and policies. It recommends that Health Authorities evaluate the work of health visitors to ascertain whether or not they are fulfilling a pro-active, not merely reactive, role.

The inquiry examines the role in terms of a three tier model of prevention. The inquiry notes the important contribution that the health visitor can make to child protection based upon knowledge of family dynamics, acceptable levels of child care and parenting and normal child development. The health visitor can act as a catalyst by collecting information from many sources. It is therefore essential that health visitors communicate the significance and consequence of their findings to colleagues who may not have the same expertise.

The inquiry notes some conflict in philosophy and expectation of the health visitor, on the one hand facilitating and supporting individuals and families requiring an open, honest and direct relationship with parents whilst ensuring other professionals were kept fully informed. On the other hand, because a health visitor is usually afforded easy access to the home there is a social policing role in relation to early identification of abuse with a view to protecting the child. This can lead to loss of parental confidence and trust. A balance must therefore be maintained between these two approaches.

Frequency of routine visiting contacts was questioned in relation to the 'short life' of Jason Plischkowsky (JP 30–31) and the health authority invited to review the adequacy of their prescribed frequency of visiting. The Doreen Aston inquiry questioned if routine visiting is achievable should more than a routine service be provided in child abuse cases? (DA 8.13)

The Carlile inquiry considers that it is appropriate for health visitors to undertake a joint visit with a social worker to investigate child abuse. (KC.95) The Lucy Gates inquiry considers the appropriateness of the health visitor role in relation to treatment and suggest that her specialism is in general health surveillance and education with only a limited responsibility in this respect. (LGP 5.52) It emphasises the role of the health visitor as a key referring-out person.

The Aston inquiry reflects on the dilemmas allocating time to child protection cases when routine visiting, more generally, is difficult to maintain. The inquiry summarises the role and the expectation of the health visitor in relation to child protection. 'Issues which need urgent debate are the type of service given to the abused child and the duties and the responsibilities of the health visitor when other agencies fail to respond. There is no doubt that health visiting objectives must focus on the safety and the welfare of the child, but the overall philosophy in relation to child protection should reflect the basic principles of health visiting. The health visitor owes a duty of care to the abused child, but this must be balanced with her duty of care to the non-abused child and other client groups.' (DA 4.34)

A number of inquiries note difficulties in maintaining health visitor contact with children who are in care (LGP 5.5.6 for example), and inquiries emphasise the need for good communication, despite and because of possible changes of workers, when children are admitted to care. This communication must be two way. (SW 1.97 1.78 LGP 5.5.6) The Carlile inquiry makes the point that the fact that a child is under the supervision or in care of another agency does not displace the continuing need for health surveillance. Indeed it should be the signal for heightened level of activity, as there must have been sound reason for the disruption of the family. (KC 165)

The role of the midwife
A number of inquiries note the value of the role of the midwife. Midwives have a significant contribution to make in the prevention of child abuse because of their antenatal contact, when they are able to observe behaviour during pregnancy and during early parenthood, which may be the first indication of risk of later abuse or neglect. Working with the health visitor they have a major role to play in enabling parents to take a responsible attitude to the care of their children to seek appropriate help and support (DA 4.47), and, where appropriate, in referring cases to the health visitor or Social Services. (RF.25 CS 6) Community midwives need clear information to assist them to work effectively. (DA 2.30) The Doreen Aston inquiry recommended that the health authority examined systems for communicating and storing information between the hospital and community midwives. The panel heard evidence that the community midwives did not perceive the procedures in existence at the time as applicable to them. The inquiry therefore recommended that health authorities ensure that every member of staff, including midwives, is conversant with the relevant child protection procedures. (DA 4.47)

General practitioners
General practitioners are responsible for the primary care of members of the community. Not only do they possess detailed knowledge of their patients and their families, their background and environment in which they live and work but also act as a link between them and other parts of the health service. (CLV 8.13.1) However a theme running through the inquiries is the isolation of the GP and the non involvement in the inter-agency system. (RF 118 CP 3.4.2) The Lucy Gates inquiry notes the need for general practitioners to move away from the narrow confines of the presented illness or injury and seize opportunities to discuss the child's welfare within a social context and the background of previous incidents and events and to provide Social Services with relevant information. (LGP 5.44)

The Reuben Carthy tragedy hinged around non reporting of injuries by a GP to Social Services. The inquiry notes that there is unfortunately substantial evidence to suggest that many general practitioners do not operate within a co-operative philosophy and are isolated from the efforts which other professionals concerned with child welfare are making to ensure good liaison and common action to protect children from abuse. It notes that it is rare for a general practitioner to attend a case conference within the child abuse procedures and expresses concern that general practitioners may fail to diagnose abuse because of the relative rarity of presentation. (RC 148–154) The Beckford inquiry reflects upon the Reuben Carthy case and heard much evidence suggesting that the general practitioners isolate themselves. (JB 235) The isolation may be two way and so that general practitioners were not always invited to case conferences. (DA)

The Kimberley Carlile inquiry discusses the general preventive role of a GP. It notes the desirability of general practitioners gaining paediatric experience and participating child health surveillance programmes. It emphasises the need for the GP to be satisfied with the developmental status of the child presented to him, as well as dealing with the presented problem, and the need for liaison with the health visitor so that home influence can be evaluated. The family practitioner committee should ensure that child abuse procedures are available to all practitioners in the area. General practitioners need to meet the same stringent standard of practice as other professionals, to fulfil their important role in a multi-disciplinary system for protecting children at risk. (KC 175) Inquiries note the need for the working arrangements of GPs to be reviewed to enable good communication between themselves and between practices and local authorities. (JC 3.4.32 DA 4.2)

Evidence was presented to the Cleveland inquiry that communication needs to flow to the general practitioners, as well. In particular emphasis was given to the need for prompt communication from hospital consultants, and good information about the child's legal status. Information should be circulated to general practitioners explaining the implications of place of safety orders and other legal powers. The matter of patient confidentiality was viewed as a consistent block to GP involvement in multi-agency frameworks. (CLV 8.13. 12–18)

Clinical medical officers
The role of the clinical medical officer is commented upon in the Doreen Aston inquiry, in relation to the developmental progress of the child. The inquiry recommends that when a proposal for a medical check arises out of the recommendation of a case conference, the chair of the conference should communicate directly with the doctor to advise the reasons for the request and to seek direct feedback. Such assessments must not take place in isolation and purposelessly. The inquiry recommends that the health authority should consider whether effectiveness of communications between each of the clinical medical officers, general practitioners and health visitors can be improved. (DA 4.53–55) There is concern about the lack of professional support for community medical officers who seemed to be isolated professionally, and who carry a heavy responsibility. (LJ 1.11) The Lucy Gates inquiry emphasises the role of a principal medical officer (child health) in the field of prevention of child abuse.

The designated doctor responsible for child protection should ensure that the clinical medical officers are fully appraised of the local procedures to protect registered children and that they maintain good communication with hospital and social service colleagues.

Community paediatricians
The developing role of community paediatricians is noted. The Lucy Gates inquiry considered that one of the most important questions to arise for the inquiry was the extent the hospital based paediatrician took responsibility for his patients. Should a paediatrician take a leadership role beyond the hospital and into the community, especially when an investigation has shown that his patient's presenting symptoms and signs arise from adverse home environment? (LGP 5.34) In evidence to the Cleveland inquiry the British Paediatric Association stressed the importance of consultant involvement in child sexual abuse with an emphasis on the continuing care of the child. The Association felt that the continuing care of children in such cases would be better provided by community paediatricians.

The inquiry noted that while there is some overlap between hospital based and community based paediatricians, the latter, are increasingly taking on tasks in child protection and in activities which are required to be carried out jointly with social workers and related to the police. (CLV 11.68)

All staff in hospital seeing children in the course of their normal duties need to be alert to the signs of child abuse. Communication within the hospital and between the hospital and community must be good.

There are examples throughout the inquiries of the failure to communicate admission to hospital to Social Services Departments. (LGC 2.9) The Lucy Gates report considers that, in addition to liaison health visitors and recording systems, there should have been direct communication between the hospital and the Social Services Department in the case of any child about whom hospital doctors and nurses felt concerned. (LGC 55.16) 'I have little doubt that part of the trouble here over communications was that some of those working in hospitals had no clear idea of the roles, powers and procedures of workers in the Social Services who needed their help and co-operation.' (LGC 55.7)

The Doreen Aston inquiry noted that the mother discharged herself from hospital the day after the birth against medical advice and could find no trace of an examination by a paediatrician. Hospital staff knew that the mother had no antenatal care, that she had had a previous cot death, that the baby was on the small side. The mother was a single parent returning to an address which she had been reluctant to disclose to hospital staff. The mother had said that she wanted a boy. It was recorded that she did not wish to speak to the social worker. 'These social factors as well as medical factors should have been taken into account before the baby left hospital.' (DA 2.24) When a paediatric assessment is requested it is important to establish that it happens. (RF 1.4)

In known risk cases a medical assessment whilst the child is still in hospital forms an important base-line, and it is important such assessment is made. It is essential that hospital doctors liaise directly with community colleagues who have responsibility for continuous oversight of health and development.

Accident and emergency departments
A particularly close relationship is needed between accident and emergency departments and local authority. The Reuben Carthy inquiry recommended that the child abuse register holders should notify the hospital of the identity of registered children, that their names should be made available to A and E department staff. (RC 62) Such departments are one of the primary places of contact between agencies and a child at risk of abuse. A senior paediatrician should be available to A and E departments in suspected cases. (LJ 118) Standard information should be included on sheets completed by examining doctors so that liaison between the department and the community is given maximum assistance (RC52), such liaison should be prompt. (LJ 11.6)

Consultant paediatrician
The consultant paediatrician may be a key figure in the diagnosis of child abuse, in the court case and in the continued surveillance of the child. The Cleveland report notes the need for paediatricians to put their diagnosis into a wider context, including the 'place of priorities and the adequacies of resources'. (CLV 8.8.33) Good communication between consultants and junior medical staff is important, as in good communication with the nurses. (CLV 8.7.52) Good communication must take place between social services and

nurses to ensure that nurses know the status of children on the ward as to whether place of safety orders have been made and generally who had custody and control of the children in question. (CLV 8.7.26)

Psychiatrists's and psychologist's contribution

The psychiatrist figures very seldom in inquiry reports in the 80s. The Beckford inquiry criticises the absence of psychiatric involvement and notes the role that a psychiatrist could have played in assessing the parents before the Beckford children were returned to them in 1982. The Lucy Gates inquiry notes that when a psychiatric assessment is needed effective communication must follow. In that case there was no report sent to the GP and no follow up child guidance made available. In Cleveland psychiatrists were used to provide second opinions. However the inquiry notes practical difficulties in providing urgent opinion because of problems psychiatrists experienced rearranging their own practices in order to be available. An unpublished report emphasises the valuable role of the psychiatrist in providing information about parents in parallel with the Social Services assessment of children. The need for good communication and a common use of language is emphasised.

Clinical psychologists may also be useful as a second opinion in child protection work. The Cleveland inquiry notes the lack of clarity on the part of the psychologist's employers about her role in relation to child sexual abuse, and the psychologist's isolation and lack of support. As in other forms of medical assessment the purpose of the psychiatric or psychological examination needs to be clear. The Cleveland inquiry notes the value of the role of psychologist in examining children where allegations of suspicions were unclear or where the abuser was known to be from outside the family. One of the paediatricians would refer all children to the clinical psychologist and, depending upon her opinion, the Social Services Department would be informed. (CLV 8.3.15) The psychiatrist and psychologist are each able to contribute to a shared opinion.

Health Service management

The inquiries describe importance of regular supervision and effective management of health visitors (see below), and the need for the health visitor to make the appropriate use of the manager (DA 2.138 for example).

There are crucial channels of communication between health visitors, nursing officers and senior community medical staff. (LGC 47.10) The Doreen Aston inquiry notes possible tensions in loyalty with the health visitor between the general practitioner and the professional line manager. It emphasises the need for rules and boundaries to be explicit and agreed. In these circumstances professional supervision of the health visitor is necessary in addition to discussions within the primary care team. The inquiry suggests that supervision should be given by a nurse manager with a health visiting background. (DA 4.15)

The Aston inquiry recommends that health authorities issue comprehensive guidelines and procedures on matters relating to child abuse, so that staff are clear about the framework in which they practise and the expectations of their employing authority. Important issues arising out of the case were: supervision of staff and of managers, presentations at case conferences, methods of following up children on the register and children causing concern, what to do when a child could not be seen, and whether to agree to visit jointly with a social worker. (DA 4.13)

Schools

There are separate aspects to the role of the school in relation to the management of the child abuse system. Firstly, to express concern about children who may be showing signs of abuse. Secondly to monitor children who are in the care of the local authority and on the child abuse register. The Beckford inquiry seeks to impress on all social agencies the value of the school as part of the management of the child abuse system. (JB 155) The Cleveland inquiry adds a third function, namely raising the awareness of children to their rights to personal safety.

Schools need to be able to recognise child abuse (LGC 18.15) and know how to report when they are concerned. The Richard Fraser inquiry commented that not all school staff had a real understanding of what procedure should be followed in the case of suspected injuries. Communication between head teachers and class teachers was problematic. When class teachers were involved in case conferences insufficient weight had been given to their views, – the ILEA Circular 81/71 stated that 'unless inappropriate or otherwise specified, the school will be best represented by the specific class teacher concerned'. (RF 88–93) The class teacher has daily contact in term-time and is in a position to see change and express concern.

The Beckford inquiry recommends that whenever a child in care is attending any educational establishment, the local authority must formally notify the education authority and the school. A letter should ask for information about non attendance and any other relevant matter pertaining to the child's health and welfare. (JB 120)

The Beckford inquiry recommended that in every school there was one member of staff who was designated as the liaison officer. In the Cleveland inquiry, it is suggested that at every school there should be male and female staff to whom children can talk about sexual matters. Such staff can help children assert their rights to personal safety.

The Education Welfare Officer (EWO)

There is concern about the role and the relationships of the EWO both with the schools and with Social Service Departments. A number of inquiries are concerned that the EWO acts as a filter for referrals from school.

There are problems transmitting referrals from head teacher to Social Services via the EWO. (LJ 13.1) The Carlile inquiry is clear that filtering of even minor concerns and filtered referral of cases to Social Services may lead to several agencies having some information and none of them possessing the whole picture. Any suspicions about child abuse must be reported by the school direct to Social Services. (KC 169 LG 13.1)

The Liam Johnson inquiry notes the expansion of the role of the EWO 'but there are uneasy grey areas around the edges'. (LJ 6.19) The inquiry makes the point that the role as 'truant officer' is not to be underestimated. 'As with so many human situations, the easy one to deal with is where the child is absent and where there is no contact and no explanation from the parents. The difficult ones are those where there are repeated periods of absence followed by short periods of attendance, or where, as here, there are plausible explanations for the absence and promises to ensure attendance are not kept.' (LJ 13.2) The inquiry notes problems in setting time limits after which all absences would be followed up, and recommends 'an overhaul of the procedures for dealing with prolonged or persistent absence particularly where attempts to contact the family are unsuccessful'. (LJ 13.2–13.4) A joint surveillance role between school teachers and EWOs has been described. (LGC 29.5)

The EWO and children under school age

The Richard Fraser inquiry notes uncertainty about the role of education welfare when a child was subject to a care order (RF 100), it also heard differing views of the involvement of the welfare service in cases of a child who is under statutory school age. This gap is also identified in the Jasmine Beckford inquiry. (JB 49) Richard Fraser's attendance at school was not pursued vigorously because he was under school age (RF 86) and the question of a developmental assessment for him was dropped because of parental resistance, being deferred until he reached school age. (RF 21) The Carlile inquiry makes the point that concern concentrated on the two children at school when it ought to have been directed towards the child to whom a nursery school place was offered, and which was rejected. (KC 212) The Beckford inquiry recommended that consideration should be given to extending the statutory duties of the education welfare office to those children under the age of 5 and attending nursery school. (JB 155)

At the end of the 80s as at the beginning, the education welfare role in relation to Social Services 'needs further consideration at a national level'. (LGP 5.21)

1.5 POLICE

Two inquiries of the early 80s, Richard Fraser and Jason Caesar note improvements in the relationships between the police and other agencies since Home Office Guidelines were issued in 1976 and DHSS Guidelines in 1980. Police forces occupy a unique role in the handling of child abuse cases. Together with the general medical practitioner and hospital authorities they provide a 24 hour a day service and they share the distinction of having the likely earliest knowledge about domestic violence and in particular physical injury to children inflicted by their parents. Over and above that, as the Beckford inquiry says, 'the police exclusively possess optimum access to a range of information about the criminal background of individuals that can be invaluable to those in agencies engaged in the assessment of child abuse. For social services and the allied agencies engaged in child care to dispense with the expertise of police officers is to indulge in self-denial that may have serious, sometimes fatal results for children at risk. (JB 159) Other enquiries emphasise various aspects of the police role yet and are critical in a number of areas.

Child protection priority

The Lucy Gates Panel report emphasises that 'where police officers visit households with young children whatever the purpose priority should be given to matters of child care and protection and any concern should be passed to colleagues who specialise in child care who will in turn advise the Social Services and other appropriate welfare agencies'. (LGP 5.4)

The Cleveland inquiry recommends that the police should recognise and develop their responsibility for the protection of the child as extending beyond the collection of evidence for court proceedings. This should include their attendance at case conferences and assistance to the other child protection agencies.

Communications

A number of inquiries comment on communication problems within the police force and between the police and other agencies. The Cleveland inquiry recommends that the police should examine their organisation to ensure there is an adequate communication network to achieve the recognition and identification of problems at operational level and assistance to develop remedies. It should also develop, monitor and maintain communication and consultation with the other agencies concerned with child protection. (CLV 247) The Liam Johnson inquiry also notes problems of communication within the police service. Cases involving suspected injury of children tend to get reported to the juvenile bureau, or now the specialist team. 'More difficult are the problems that arise when the police investigate a crime involving the parents which indicates a lifestyle which might be detrimental to the children, for example drug abuse or prostitution, or where they may be caught in the cross fire of domestic violence between parents. Such incidents may or may not get reported to police officers with responsibility for protecting children from abuse. Again there is a filtering mechanism at work which means that all these incidents do not necessarily get passed on to the Social Services.' (LJ 6.31–34)

Criminal and care proceedings

It was requested in the Cleveland inquiry that the police have been rightly concerned with the evidential questions raised by the conflict of medical opinion and the effect of it upon criminal proceedings. It is an important element but not the only or paramount one for consideration. The Police failed to give sufficient weight to the responsibilities of the Social Services Department after a diagnosis of sexual abuse had been made and their statutory duty toward the child. In complying with this statutory duty and where they believed a child's welfare required it, the Social Services Department had to obtain a court order in order to deal with the child appropriately. The civil evidential requirements both in Juvenile Court proceedings and in wardship are different from the criminal courts and the standard of proof is not as high. The social workers therefore were not only entitled to proceed in cases where the police felt unable to act but had a duty to the child to do so. This duty may not always have been fully appreciated by the police.' (CLV 6.78) The Karl McGoldrick report provides another view. 'A sufficient level of 'proof' may not be obtained as a result of (police) inquiries to allow them to initiate actions but doubts when suspicions can remain . . . although one of the agencies involved in child abuse inquiries, they face constraints that are not present in a lot of other agencies. They require a higher level of 'proof'.' (KMcG 7.1)

There can be misunderstanding about investigative roles and the Cleveland inquiry noted that the police felt that social workers appeared not to understand the constraints upon the police in conducting investigations and instigating criminal proceedings. In the regrettable absence of any consultative process and the discussions between police and Social Services, the different approaches and perceptions of both agencies were not appreciated by the other. (CLV 6.36)

There is a need for police involvement in the child protection process yet a number of reports describe the non involvement of the police at critical stages and as well as various points of tension.

Non access

At no time were the police involved in the Kimberley Carlile case. That report identifies two particular roles for the police. 'If a social worker has any difficulty in obtaining access to a child in pursuit of a statutory duty to investigate cases, where information is received which suggests that there are grounds for care proceedings, the police must be informed. The police will then investigate, in collaboration with Social Services. Between them a decision will be made whether to revisit the place where the child is thought to be, or apply for a warrant which is executable by the police.' (KC 172–174) Secondly, where anonymous calls from neighbours are involved. 'There may be particular help that the police can give in tracing and even interviewing the caller as well as accompanying social workers.' The inquiry notes that the child abuse procedures in Greenwich refer to the role of the police only in connection with their participation in case conferences. It recommends that this should be amplified to include police involvement, where and when appropriate, in the investigative stages. (KC 100)

The Richard Fraser inquiry referred to the failure to involve the police as 'a crucial error in affecting Richard's future'. (RF 59) The Beckford inquiry notes that had the police been involved more fully the police might have carried out further investigation, not merely with view to pressing criminal charges but also, more validly for the purposes of child protection, to providing the necessary profile of the battering Beckford parents.

Joint interviews

The Cleveland report notes that with the increased awareness of the problem of sexual abuse of younger children within the family, the need for a more complex and sensitive type of inter-agency intervention and co-operation required alterations of existing arrangements. It notes that the Police were slow to respond to this need. (CLV 12.13)

Case conferences

The primary task of the police is to investigate crime. The Joint Circular from the DHSS and the Home Office states the hope that where a case conference has been held 'chief officers of police (while retaining the capacity to take independent action) will take into account any views expressed by the conference on the effect on an investigation on the welfare of the child'.

The importance of police attending case conferences is much noted (TH 10.9. LGP 4.27 for example). While it may be unnecessary for police to attend all case conferences and statutory reviews, where there was an important step being contemplated in the placement of children who have been abused by their parents, it is crucial for the police to be present. Yet invitations as a matter of course do not seem to happen (DA 2.213 for example). The Jason Caesar inquiry considers DHSS guidance on police involvement in case conferences (1976). The involvement of the police can represent a considerable threat to the confidential relationship between practitioner and client which is the basis of medical and social work practice since it is normally the duty of the police, to follow up information, however obtained, which indicates criminal activity. Police follow up may lead to breakdown in co-operation or practitioners for holding information. (JC 3.4.7)

The police role in the protection of children will continue to be an ancillary to the work of the Social Services Department where the statutory responsibility remains, and not a substitute for it. In particular, when planning for surviving children, or dealing with other disrupted family situations it is important that the police recognise the limitations of their expertise as well as their strengths. (LJ 8.21)

Confidentiality

Toward the end of the 80s two inquiries, Tyra Henry and Liam Johnson discuss in detail the matter of confidentiality in relation to the police. Disclosure of previous convictions to case conferences is a problem impeding real inter-agency co-operation. (LJ 12.5) The main difficulty, it suggests, is that 'the police have traditionally regarded and still regard the information in their hands as more confidential than the confidential information possessed by other agencies'. It goes on to recommend that the same conventions around confidentiality described in 'Working Together' relating to the medical profession should also apply to the police. (LJ 7.21)

However, that the need for understanding about the communication of information should be two way. 'It is important for representatives of other agencies to appreciate that when a police investigation is in its early stages harm may be done in disclosing all the details of the progress of the investigation particularly where there are areas of particular weakness to the case.'

Court liaison

The Liam Johnson inquiry emphasises the importance of liaison so that sufficient information is given to the court dealing with bail to ensure bail conditions are consistent with other court orders. (LJ 7.50–53) Officers dealing with bail applications should have sufficient information about any other court orders in relation to the child to enable them to place it before the court and ensure that any bail conditions are not inconsistent with those orders. The same inquiry notes that the police and the Crown Prosecution Service have a particular responsibility to try and ensure that the prosecution of offenders takes place as soon as possible. (LJ 12.2 see also below)

Media

Three inquiries note problems in relation to the police and the media over the fact of the child abuse inquiries themselves and the consequence for local working relationships. (CLV 6.64. LGC 20.6. LJ 7.27–33).

1.6 PROBATION SERVICE

Probation officers may become involved in cases of child abuse either through their responsibility for the supervision of offenders against children, or as a result of their responsibility to the court for the supervision of children. A number of inquiries identify the need for frequent and open communication when a probation officer may identify a case of child abuse or suspected child abuse. (KC 170–172 JC 3.4.18)

The Charlene Salt and Jason Caesar inquiries both describe a role for the probation officer working with the parent separate from, or at a distance from, the child care issues. However, the Tyra Henry inquiry notes that the Inner London Probation Service accepted a primary role in the detection of child abuse. It emphasises the need for a close link between the care plan for the child and the social inquiry report about the mother. It emphasises that the probation service should not have proceeded to make recommendations to the court which would affect the child's future without asking Social Services whether the revised care plan still stood in view of the criminal proceedings. Where necessary the probation service should ask for a recall of the case conference. The inquiry makes the point that in care and child abuse cases, the probation service should be involved in the process of exchanging and evaluating information and should not be confined to an observing or reactive role. This was fully recognised in the Service's submission of evidence, but its practical application needed attention. (TH 10.6)

An unpublished report stresses the need for the task of probation volunteers to be clearly defined and limited. This should be confined to 'befriending' and not include tasks appropriate for professional workers. Volunteers should be supervised by agencies and their status clearly defined.

SECTION 2 ISSUES FOR MANAGEMENT

This section considers a number of aspects of the organisational context of professional practice. On the basis of an individual case, except where specific failures of decision making or systems process are identifiable, the inquiries find it difficult to draw conclusions about the performance of the workers and the performance of the organisation.

Organisations change and so do the demands made upon them. At the beginning of the 80s the Lucy Gates reports said 'The period of 1969 to 1979 saw substantial changes nationally in the organisation of services and the roles of personnel. It was marked by the ending of the specialised Child Care Services of the Children's Departments and the evolution of generic social work in the new Social Services Departments. The actions of individuals and services must be judged against the background of these developments'. (LGC 22.2) 'We find that in most instances such failures (of practice, interpretation and judgement by individuals) are concerned with deficiencies in professional and in service training, professional supervision and management, problems arising from the organisation of services and policies and procedures both local and more general.' (LGP 6.16) But the criticism continued.

In 1987 the Kimberley Carlile inquiry was noting 'an inherently defective multi-disciplinary system' – 'This inherently defective system was made even less fully functional by the special circumstances in Greenwich during 1985–6, of recurring resource restraints of a rate-capped London borough, of reduced staffing levels due to key members leaving, of disarray of the community health services, and of a sudden increase in reported cases of children at risk which was the common experience across the country.' (KC 210) 'We recommend that all such Social Services Departments fundamentally review the organisation of their services, and the distribution of their resources, to make sure that they are as well equipped as possible to deal with this trend. (KC 72)

The theme of disruption in services following substantial departmental change and reorganisation was noted in the previous report of child abuse inquiries. The way in which Social Services Departments and health authorities cope with the implementation of the Children Act, and Community Care legislation provides a major challenge to the effective delivery of all the services provided by these organisations. The impact of this reorganisation on output and outcome of work for child protection and child care, needs the most careful monitoring and regulation.

The major themes drawn from the inquiries are the real difficulties of structures, competing priorities within agencies, and difficulties of relationship between agencies. Structural problems are compounded by the effects of lack of resources.

2.1 THE ROLE OF SENIOR MANAGEMENT

The inquiries, generally, do not make clear what they believe to be the responsibilities of senior management. In one respect the Cleveland inquiry is different. 'The failure to resolve problems and co-ordinate action at middle and senior management levels in both organisations increased difficulties of social workers and the police on the ground.' 'In such a circumstance, it must fall to the responsibility of the respective chief officers to build bridges and trust between the two services.' (CLV 4.186) Interaction at senior level can mirror interaction in other parts of the organisation, or actually make things worse. In the circumstance of problems at the top, the ACPC was unable to resolve the crisis itself. A priority for senior management, therefore, is the establishment of effective relationships with other agencies.

A hurdle to cross for senior managers as all others, is the different points of view derived from differing agencies functions. One point of tension is how to relate 'bureaucratic' to 'professional' structures. For example the Director of Social Services in Cleveland told the inquiry of a meeting with paediatricians. 'The existing resources could not cope with the number of referrals and I wondered whether there was any way in which they could reduce diagnoses to allow us to obtain the resources which would enable us to provide a proper service for children and families. The doctors said that this was not professionally acceptable to them and that other services needed to realise that this was a major development in child health which required an appropriate new initiative . . .' (CLV 4.117–118).

'Creating the right atmosphere'

'A really effective social work service can only be achieved where the council through its Social Services Policy Committee and senior management provide the resources, create the atmosphere and establish the policies and procedures, through which the department's statutory responsibilities can be carried out.' (SW 10.1 also DA 3.15–18)

A number of reports refer to the need for a clear policy framework for child protection work, and the need for policy to be known and understood. A theme is the need to balance prevention against protection in such policy. The Kimberley Carlile inquiry made the point that Greenwich's Child Care Policy, emphasising prevention, did not play sufficient emphasis on the protection of children, and it recommended that local authorities review their child care policies from this point of view. (KC 80) A similar point was made in the Lucy Gates Panel report which suggested that Bexley Social Services Department misunderstood their statutory responsibilities in child care and protection. 'Social workers and their superiors argue that they had a statutory duty to prevent the Gates children entering and remaining in care. In general terms this is correct . . . . . But this legislation (1963 Act) was never intended to mean that preventive work takes priority over voluntary reception into care or other powers to secure the protection and welfare of children.' (LGP 3.1 see also CLV 4.13–4.15)

Conflicts in setting priorities between competing demands is noted though not explored. A number of reports comment on difficulties of prioritisation of services in Social Services Departments. The Cleveland report notes the local authority decision taken in 1985 to give child care priority over other services, and the consequent changes and improvements in services made the following year. (CLV 4.6–7) However the Liam Johnson inquiry expressed concern that priority had been given to providing a duty service to those who come in with problems requiring social work help, which meant that 'the social workers priorities are determined by the public who come in rather than the social workers themselves' (LJ 10.13) and the Emma Jane Hughes inquiry expresses concern that insufficient priority was given to the case bearing in mind the local authorities statutory responsibilities.

The Aston inquiry related prioritisation to resources: 'Responsibility laid with the management team in Area 8 to establish priorities within the resources available and to ensure that work undertaken was done to a satisfactory level. Nonetheless the Council and senior management should have ensured that the process by which resources were allocated was seen to be based on clearly established priorities ... If statutory services are to be sustained at a safe standard Central Government needs to note the cumulative effect of rate capping'. (DA 3.14).

In the context of a review of health visiting functions the Aston inquiry recommends that Health Authorities responsible for planning, managing and providing the health visiting service should determine the kind and level of service to be offered to the local populations. 'They should set out in a written policy document the objectives and key tasks for the health visiting service as a whole, generally and in relation to child protection. Specific targets and priorities for the service and individual health visitors and managers should be established, to ensure that they are working in accordance with their Code of Practice'. (DA 4.33 see also JB 14)

Setting standards and monitoring action – the gaps between policy and practice

Inquiries describe the need for senior management to establish standards and monitor them, a process which effectively can fill the gap between a central policy and everyday practice.

The Gates Panel report questions whether there were any effective policies and practises for nursing staff developed in relation to the care and surveillance of children at risk in Bexley (5.69) and reflects upon failures to follow procedures in Bexley. It describes 'the gap between the circulation of national advice and the advocacy of ideal procedures and the reality of everyday practice, when overworked practitioners endeavour to cope with their workloads'. (LGP 4.24)

The Panel draws attention to the fact that it is still not mandatory for social workers to be trained or qualified before undertaking statutory child care work (LGP 5.101), and there appears to be no means of ensuring that knowledge of social workers engaged in statutory work conforms to minimum standards. There is no system for deciding what amount of work can safely be undertaken by social workers without jeopardising the quality of work to individual clients. (LGP 5.103)

'In an attempt to ensure a consistent level of professional practice throughout the department, senior management are to establish a monitoring system within the system resources. Existing procedures are to be reexamined and rewritten where necessary to ensure that these instructions embody legal and regulatory requirements and reflect the standard of care expected in relation to each foster child.' (EJH press statement)

'Policy should define the lowest level of what is acceptable. In the 'A' case, Social Services staff tolerated practices which in some instances they knew to be unacceptable because of the demands that their own agency was making on the foster home. The new Boarding Out Regulations will change this, but again we stress that the full implementation of these regulations is essential.' ('A' 8)

Monitoring is essential in this and clear policies are the basis of effective monitoring of output. The Tyra Henry inquiry was troubled 'by the fact that the inadequacies of the case conferences on Tyra Henry were not picked up at any high level. There is of course a limit to how much vetting of individual cases can be done by senior management but there is also a responsibility at these levels not only to lay down rules but to see whether and how they are working'. (TH 6.21) The Cleveland inquiry makes a recommendation along similar lines: 'senior managers in Social Services Departments need to ensure that they have efficient systems available to allow accurate monitoring of service activity which will alert them to problems that need to be resolved'. (CLV 247) The Cleveland inquiry recommends that Social Services Departments establish information systems in relation to child protection. The system would relate to the initiating report, the investigation, action, and control (by Social Services and the courts) establishing such a system would involve establishing a minimum level of standard, and allow monitoring of outcome in relation to it.

Establishing complaints procedures

The Lucy Gates Panel report emphasises the need for the establishment of effective complaints procedures. It recommends that there should be a more universally understood and accepted system of dealing with complaints on child abuse cases within the statutory and voluntary child care agencies. It suggests that a more coherent system is required so that those with complaints can easily learn how to complain; what happened to the complaint; and the outcome of any investigation. (LGP 7.15) The 'Working Together' guideline echoes the need to complaints procedures and should lead to the establishment of effective complaints procedures within child protection agencies.

The maintenance of an organisation

The inquiries do not consider the optimum shape or size of an organisation to undertake effective child protection work. Neither do they consider the type of organisation that can best accommodate a specialist child abuse consultant or specialist child protection teams. The establishment of the role of child abuse co-ordinator is discussed below (see 3.5), as is the establishment of effect court liaison and legal advisory network (see 4.6).

Inquiries do note the disruptive, chaotic, consequence of National Health Service reorganisation. (LGC 4.8 & KC 121) The Carlile inquiry notes that 'the last six months of Kimberley Carlile's life unfortunately coincided with the delayed effect of the reorganisation of National Health Service in 1982. Case loads of health visitors were heavy. The turnover of staff was high, and morale low. Inevitably, development of an effective service became stultified at a time when the number of child abuse cases calling for health visiting action was increasing'. (KC 121)

In addition, a number of inquiries discuss the decentralisation of Social Services Departments into neighbourhood or patch teams. The Shirley Woodcock inquiry notes that the process was disruptive and in the period which the area inquiry team considered, chaotic (SW 3.4 for example).

The Carlile inquiry urges in relation to decentralisation that 'it must be acknowledged how fragile isolated teams can be, so that, if they are to provide emergency and statutory services, failsafe mechanisms must be established to safe guard the service, for example at times of staff shortage'. (KC 73)

The Tyra Henry inquiry identifies the management task in all of this and returns to 'creating the right climate': ' . . . procedures need to take account of what we can best describe as a culture of an area office in a decentralised Social Services structure. We believe that local cultures deserve study and that much that went wrong in Tyra's case may be traceable to an office culture which permitted it and possibly encouraged it to happen. The relative autonomy of each area can lead to the development of idiosyncratic practices such as the effective overlooking of the statutory view of children who are both at risk and are in care ... (It) is the directorate's task without breaching the independence of the areas, to deter this happening ... Tedious things like check lists may be indispensable for this purpose'. (TH 6.11 also LGC 68.2, 69.5)

Clear levels of decision making

Clarity of decision making is an essential component of Child Protection Practice. In so far as inquiries refer to the decision making processes within the local authority it tends to be in terms of uncertainty, and the need for improvement. However the inquiries say very little about intra-agency decision making and tend to attribute to case conferences a decision making authority, whilst at the same time tending also to note that case conferences make recommendations and not decisions.

The Tyra Henry inquiry considers the role of members in the review of individual cases. It notes that 'the ultimate legal responsibility for children in care lies on the body of elected councillors .... The need for access to central authority in situations such as we are considering is especially great in a decentralised electorate where the counter part of relative autonomy is relative isolation and when making do with getting by can become a way of life'. (TH 9.2) The inquiry represents the need for a spread of responsibility offering necessary support to social workers who are at the sharp end of child abuse. The inquiry does not, as it might have, consider the implications for the users of services, parents and children, of this role of the elected member.

When second level managers are referred to as involved in decision making, the extent of their authority tends to be unclear (for example CH 3.4.3). References to area managers role in decision making as chairs of case conferences masks a discussion of their role as decision makers in the discharge of the statutory responsibilities of the local authority.

A theme running through the inquiries, however, is that in whatever the first and second line managers decide about cases, they should do so on the basis of full information and take a probing rather than passive role. How decisions are made in relation to statutory responsibilities in local authorities appears to be in need of further study. Particularly so, the relationship between intra-agency delegation of authority and decision making and inter-agency case conference processes.

The critical role of the first line manager

The relationship between field worker and first line manager/ supervisor is a critical relationship in the management of child protection case. In the same way that the field worker is at the interface between client and agency, the first line manager is the field workers' route to resources, and decisions which need a higher level of authority; the field workers' reference point in case planning and review; and is a check on the individuals' performance and conduct.

All the inquiries regard supervision as essential and refer to it in particular in relation to field social workers and health visitors. There seems however to be a blurring of the role of first line managers – which of their tasks are 'management', and which 'supervision', and how do they relate. It is unclear from the inquiries the extent to which agencies in these cases address this issue, and develop policies on the supervision of the staff.

The primary role of the nurse manager is to facilitate staff professionally so that they are able to deliver a high standard of service. In relation to the health visitor an essential component of the role is monitoring and evaluating the standard of service delivered through, among other methods, supervision. Effective supervision should involve the nurse manager in assuring that the health visitor is making a meaningful contribution to the inter-agency child protection plan. This might involve establishing a sequence of events in order to provide the basis for analyzing the case and structuring the health visitors work within clear objectives. (DA 4.37) The report notes that supervision in these terms was beyond the capacity of the nurse managers in the authorities considered. It is not possible to be carried out for the number of staff for whom the nurse manager was responsible. (DA 4.37)

Responsibilities of team leaders

The Aston inquiry is helpful in describing the range of responsibilities of team leaders in addition to the personal supervision of staff. These included setting work priorities within the overall statutory framework, together with policies and practices laid down by the Social Services Committee and the Director of Social Services. (DA 3.23–25)

The Tyra Henry inquiry puts its finger with emphasis on the importance of the team leader function. 'A serious error of judgement which gets past this point may become entrenched in the management of the case. We recommend that the function of team leader should be reassessed with the view of treating and teaching team leadership as a skill and in particular to training team leaders in techniques of supervision. The relevant features must include means of double checking important judgements capable of influencing the long-term management of child care cases.' (TH 7.13) In view of the recurrent themes of this report of checking judgement and of purposeful planning, this recommendation stands as one the most important on any subject in any of the inquiries.

2.2 SUPERVISION

The supervision of social workers

The use of personal skills within a structured supervisory context is a recurrent theme in the inquiries. The scope of field social worker is such that they need to be trained 'to cope with multiple roles enabling them to provide both support and practical help to full range of clients, and to combine this role with one of surveillance and protection, as in the case of child protection. On occasions, when the reasons for involving with the client change, the role similarly changes. This inevitably gives rise to potential conflict, both within the social worker and between the social worker and the client, and the social worker needs to be able to recognise and deal with it'. (JC 3.3) Yet the Kimberley Carlile quotes the Social Services Inspectorate report of March 1986 entitled 'Inspection of the supervision of social workers in the assessment and the monitoring of cases of child abuse when children, subject of a court order, have been returned home' which states that 'no Social Services Department had a clear and explicit written policy statement about the nature of supervision, and no authority prescribed the method of supervision in detail'. (KC 188) The findings of the inquiry into Mr and Mrs 'A' confirms this. Such a policy should deal with difficult issues such as what happens when there is a breakdown of confidence between supervisor and supervisee, how collusion between the two is to be avoided, what part the checking of records, the observations and the testing of client satisfaction should have.

There are also questions raised by our investigation by the proper role for a supervisor prior to and in a case conference. ('A' 7)

Inquiries describe the need for effective supervision of second and first line managers. (LJ 10.12 EJH 8.3.1 and DA 3.45 for example) And a further point is made in both the Beckford and Carlile cases that the key worker was also undertaking managerial functions. In the Carlile case this was a team leader. 'We doubt if an assistant director can be reasonably expected to provide the kind of time and attention a supervisor of child abuse cases might need from his superior. This is a compelling reason that leads us to recommend that team managers should not carry child abuse cases. That will avoid the unfortunate impact of dislocation in management.' (KC 186)

Supervision of health visitors

There is a need for suitably qualified and experienced managers regarding the nursing officer. The Carlile inquiry says 'she was new in the post, was overwhelmed by her work load, and lack of preparedness for the task of supervising the health visitor in a child abuse case'. (KC 22 see also LGC 26 and LCP 5.65) The Beckford inquiry identifies the differences between the relationship of a health visitor and her line manager to that of the social worker and her line manager. The inquiry strongly recommends 'that the practice and planning of regular discussions between the health visitors and senior nurses should be established and the nurses should particularly ensure that they discuss all child abuse cases regularly with the health visitor involved, even if she herself does not consider that there is any problem with which she is unable to deal'. (JB 220)

The Aston inquiry recommended that health authorities 'ensure that formal systems exist at all levels of nurse management whereby professional supervision is afforded priority and sufficient time built in to enable the process . . . . . Additional supervision should be provided to newly qualified health visitors'. (DA 4.43)

Purposes of supervision

The supervisor must establish that the worker has the knowledge and skills to carry out the task. (JB 215) It is important to ensure that the work load covered by the field worker does not reach a level which would prevent the social worker from visiting clients in accordance with the plan and the appropriate timetable. (JB 217)

Inquiries emphasise the need for planning to be undertaken in the supervisory context and note the absence of it (LGC 37.23 and DA 3.37 for example).

A key purpose of supervision is to ensure that plans are carried out, and that agency policies and procedures are implemented (SW 5.39, LGP 5.1.1.3 and JK 2.29 for example). And other inquiries identify the need to monitor the quality of record keeping in supervision (SW 6.18 for example). The Carlile inquiry adds a different point of emphasis to the purpose of supervision, related to ensuring that the work is done. 'We recommend that supervision should make sure that certain action is taken in a way of capable of evaluated within a specified time scale.' (KC 192–5)

An unpublished Social Services Department report is clear about the decision making role in this aspect of the relationship. Potential deviation from the prerequisite laid down plan must be considered by the manager with overall responsibility for the case. Equally it follows that any potential deviation from the pattern of involvement by other agencies incorporated in the plan must also be reported to and discussed with the team manager with overall responsibility.

A further purpose of supervision is to provide objectivity and critical analysis. The Carlile inquiry quotes the Social Services Inspectorate 'The purpose of professional supervision must be to help (field workers) provide the most appropriate form of service for the client and to assist workers to maintain their objectivity'. (KC 190) There are examples of failure to do this. (LGC 37.11) It is important to identify the attitude of social workers towards the case (JB 217) and help the social worker recognise the effect achieved by the emotions being beamed out from the family. It is also a process which enables practitioners to know themselves. (KC 192) as The method and process of supervision can militate against the achievement of objectivity and thorough analysis by the worker, with critical consequences. The Carlile inquiry also identifies as a purpose of supervision the provision of a second opinion. (KC 192–195)

A purpose of supervision is also to provide support. 'The work is stressful and it is important that their personal needs are not overlooked.' (CLV 247) However experienced a worker, it is possible to get stuck, confused, frightened or bored. The task of supervision is to be watchful for these signs and even contemplate reallocating the case if the case is overwhelming the social worker (KC 192–5 and JB 217 for example). An integral part of offering support is a capacity to 'allow' into supervision information from practitioners when they are not able to undertake tasks in line with departmental procedures. 'Of particular interest is the emphasis given to the responsibility of practitioners in exercising their accountability to ensure that the reality of their practice is made known to and understood by appropriate persons or authorities. If genuinely held concerns are expressed they should not attract censure.' (DA 3.48)

Finally supervision should provide praise. 'What seems to us to be lacking, is positive praise for good work. The point has been made to us more than once during this inquiry that particularly for social workers, no one praises you for good pieces of work, they only blame you when things go wrong. It does seem to us that management should have a role in this.' (LJ 8.35)

Methods of supervision

Supervision is an integral part of case management. The method of supervision must systematically and formally review work done against purposes, and identify how perceptions and feelings may be affecting work done, whether between field worker and family, or field worker and supervisor. 'Positive and consistent supervision was needed to ensure that her management of her case was loyal to the care order and not to her private estimation of Claudette Henry's needs.' (TH 7.9 also JB 118)

Inquiries emphasise that supervision should be formal and pro-active. The Kimberley Carlile inquiry quotes the Social Services Inspectorate which noted that supervisors could use their time more effectively if they resisted the temptation to be drawn into reactive supervision and spent more of their time on planned work, focused on stated objectives. 'Supervision calls for an initiative from the supervisor. It must be pro-active, and not just reactive.' (JB 142–3) Part of this is to see and sign records (CP 7.6 for example) and if necessary undertake joint visiting. (TH 7.10)

The Tyra Henry inquiry emphasises the need for 'interventionist and challenging supervision'. We recognise that the prescription for supervision of this character is potentially disruptive and that it needs careful working out and sensitive application'. (TH 7.12)

The Aston inquiry recognises the pressures on team leaders on Lambeth and Southwark in trying to accord proper priority to supervision whilst coping with rising work loads, vacancies, and shortage of administrative support. (DA 3.43) 'Supervision for newly qualified social workers needs to be frequent so as to provide support; informative, in the sense of supplementing the knowledge of the worker; regular so as to ensure that goals are being pursued; motivating to stretch the worker's skills and develop the confidence – in other words, FIRM . . . . . Whilst child abuse cases necessarily produce strong emotional reaction which require a supportive element in supervision, the worker also derives support from ensuring that goals for the protection for the child have been set and that progress is being monitored.' (DA 3.40 also LGP 5.113)

2.3 COMMITMENT TO TRAINING

The previous analysis of child abuse inquiries reflected on the allocation of cases to unqualified workers. That is not a theme in inquiries of the 80s. However there are numerous examples of cases being allocated to staff who are newly qualified and inexperienced in child protection work. This is most commonly commented upon in relation to social workers and health visitors (for example LGC 24.3. JB 46. LGP 5.98 and others). There are two instances of cases being allocated to students, not commented adversely upon in the inquiries. (CP 3.4.1 & CH 2.11) There are also examples of supervisors and team managers new into post not having had experience of child abuse work. (LGC 24.3 & DA 2.50)

The Cleveland inquiry heard evidence from BASW in relation to child sexual abuse warning against 'the danger of creating an illusion of knowledge that does not exist'. (CLV 13.32) More tangibly the Tyra Henry inquiry guards against wrong assumptions of expertise. 'The choice of a key social worker is in many cases influenced, and sometimes determined, by the known interests, experience and possibly training of the available personnel. There is a general risk that expertise which is needed in many fields of social work will be treated as being available when it is not, or that it will not be available when it is needed.' (TH 7.20)

Levels of skill

Agencies need to know which skills that are available, and which need to be developed. Cumbria Social Services Department reported to the McGoldrick Panel that 'the Department needed a period of change covering 4–5 years to enable staff working in the area to develop the necessary attitudes and skills to allow working practices to move forward'. (KMcG.28)

Gaps in the training of all the disciplines involved in child protection are identified and minimum levels of skill to be derived from social work and health visiting courses are commented about in a number of inquiries. The Lucy Gates inquiry also comments upon the need for training in child abuse and violence in the family as part of the undergraduate medical education. (LGP 5.45)

The nature of the problem is identified in the London Borough of Southwark's submission to the Doreen Aston inquiry in which they stated that 'it was their normal practice that professionally qualified social workers were allocated child abuse cases within a few months of starting work and if they could not operate in that way it was highly likely that a significant number of child abuse cases would be unallocated'. The Panel believed that 'this raises the significant issue of the expectation on Social Services Department about the training on child abuse received in the certificate of qualification of social work'. (DA 3.29–30)

The Lucy Gates inquiry Panel expressed concern about the lack of knowledge on the part of some social workers and their managers in relation to: the law on child protection; the identification of child abuse; the physical and emotional development of children; the physical and emotional needs of children. (LGP 6.12)

The Carlile inquiry noted the need for employers and those providing training to work closely together. An intersection point is needed – 'we recommend that CCETSW should oversee continuing discussions between those organising courses and employers to dovetail their respective responsibilities for the standard of service provided to clients'. (KC 183) It recommends that agreement is reached concerning the minimum expectations of the social worker at the point of qualification. (KC 179)

The Beckford inquiry believed that if the length of courses cannot be increased wider training should be offered in the form of post qualification modules. (JB 200) Other inquiries consider that post qualification specialist training in addition to basic professional training should be a prerequisite of undertaking child protection work. (LGP 6.19 & HK 7.10) At the very least the 'A' inquiry recommended, the Department should ensure that 'hence forward only a qualified social worker should have responsibility for managing statutory child care cases. ('A' 10)

The Tyra Henry inquiry addressed a particular training issue. 'The problem of 'positive' racial stereo-types needs to be fully addressed both in the training of social workers (and associated professionals too) and in a more considered deployment of black social workers to work with black families. We are not thinking of racial matching or anything like it in making the latter part of this recommendation. We are concerned to ensure, where there is doubt or difficulty about cultural aspects of behaviour of lifestyle, the input and evaluation of a social worker of similar background.' (TH 7.8)

The direction and content of post-qualifying and in-service training

The reports comment on training in both statutory and voluntary agencies, their field workers and their supervising staff.

A number of inquiries emphasise the need for training to be provided after qualification on an inter-agency basis. Inquiries emphasise the need for training in working together and the merit of training in confidentiality and recording in an inter-agency context. The ACPC is seen as having an important co-ordinating role in this (see Section 4 below). (See CP 7.3–4, RF 132, KC 165 and HK 7.8 for examples).

The Cleveland inquiry makes a series of recommendations in relation to training. 'Training is one of the major needs shown by the Cleveland experience. We recognise that training requirements are different for each profession . . . . . There is a need for inter-agency training and recognition of the role of other disciplines. For example police officers and social workers designated to interview children should have joint training in their approach to this task.' (CLV 251–2)

Social work training

The need to train managers, in particular first line managers is identified. '(All) new first line managers (should be) provided with an appropriate induction programme and management training. The contents of the training provided for these managers, we believe, should concentrate on the general management training, employment legislation and industrial relations, leadership skills, team building, setting priorities and attainable objectives, evaluation and how to give good supervision (including knowledge of legal provisions and departmental procedures).' (KC 185 also LGP 6.13)

A number of inquiries emphasise the need for training in the chairmanship of case conferences. (TH 7.14 also KMcG 75 and others)

As noted, inquiries emphasise the need for a training in the legal framework. (also LJ 16.3 and SW 5.39) Inquiries relating to the deaths of children in foster care have paid particular attention to the needs for training in statutory duties derived from the Boarding Out Regulations, and in aspects of fostering assessment and matching (SW 5.39. EJH press statement) Inquiries identify the training needs of other Social Services staff, home helps (LGC 24.9) and day nursery staff in the recognition of sexual abuse. (RF 73)

The Tyra Henry inquiry identifies two further training needs for social workers. The first is that in the training practice and supervision of social workers, systematic attention should be paid to affects of bereavement, separation and loss. The second is awareness in both how the presence of racism affects people in society (and) how this process itself affects the demands of social work practice. (TH 7.8 and 7.11)

Medical training

The medical profession needs to appreciate the legal implications of and the responsibility for the evidential requirements of their work. (CLV 252) The training needs of the medical profession is noted in other respects: more teaching in the emotional and the psychological aspects of child neglect and injuries to the child (RF 135); and the recognition of child abuse in all aspects. (KMcG 74)

A number of inquiries recommend the development of training for general practitioners. For example the Reuben Carthy inquiry recommends that the Family Practitioner Committee is encouraged 'to include in the vocational training skills for general practitioners education in child abuse, and procedures relating therefore. (RC 153 see also KMcG 75. LGC 26.3) The Lucy Gates Panel inquiry recommends that the general practitioners should receive specific information and training with regard to the role of the health visitor and that of the social worker. Primary health care should not be set up until the role of these workers has been clarified by the practice. (LGP 5.45)

The need for training of junior medical staff in hospitals, in particular accident and emergency departments, is emphasised. This training should include 'recognition and the need for a careful comprehensive history, examination and documentation of injuries'. (KMcG 74–75 and LJ 8.10) The Johnson and McGoldrick inquiries also recommend that this training is undertaken in conjunction with other agencies! (The) hospital is not isolated from the community, and if anything the doctors there need more information about the role and procedures of the other agencies than is the case of those who are working in the care of the community services'. (LJ 8.14)

Training for nurses and health visitors

The Beckford inquiry and the Aston inquiry in particular consider health visitor training. The Beckford inquiry concluded 'that while there is a general and unspecified awareness among health visitors of the children at risk of abuse, field workers are not always knowledgable about specific factors relating to child abuse'.
(JB 208–10)

The Aston inquiry recommended 'that training about child protection is rooted in the inter-agency context. Shared learning with students on other courses, ie. social work, probation, would be beneficial'. It goes on to recommend 'that during the period of field work and supervised practice, the health visitor is involved with child abuse, suspected child abuse and case conferences, if such experience can be gained within the training district. During the first year after qualification a health visitor should receive frequent supervision by a qualified health visitor manager both individually and in a peer group of recently qualified health visitors'. (DA 4.19–21)

The Aston and Johnson inquiries recommend training for nurse managers. (LJ 11.12) The Aston recommends that nurse managers should receive training in supervision, particularly in child abuse work and be given the time and opportunity to carry out the function effectively. (DA 4.39) A number of inquiries emphasise the need for continuing education training for health visitors. The McGoldrick inquiry recommends the health visitor should receive specific training for their role in management of families involved in child abuse, and the Beckford inquiry thinks it important that health authority should ensure that health visitors should understand 'the policy for child abuse'. (KMcG 79. JB 208–210)

Training of police

The Heidi Koseda inquiry was anxious that the police recognise the special skills which staff and other agencies perceive them to have. 'Alone among the agencies involved the police have the duty to prevent crime and to detect and investigate criminal offences and are universally perceived as having expertise therein. It is therefore essential that officers who assist other agencies in difficult or complex cases such as this do have the training and experience to discharge this function.' (HK 4.12 also 4.13)

The Cleveland inquiry recommends that the police training needs to be developed well beyond the acquisition of knowledge in respect of criminal offences involved. It also comments too on the need for training for lawyers. All lawyers engaged in this type of work including judges and magistrates should have a greater awareness of, and inform themselves about, the nature of child abuse and the management of children subjected to abuse and in particular sexual abuse. (CLV 252 also JB 2.210)

Training related to resources

The Beckford, Carlile and Cleveland inquiries urge that money is made available for post qualification training. It should be a set proportion of Social Services expenditure on staffing. (KC 184) The Beckford inquiry addresses the fact that social work training needs to be extended and its conclusion is that '. . . political commitment and support to this development, and generally to educating and training social workers must carry a high priority in public spending'.
(JB 197) The Liam Johnson inquiry pinpoints an underlying problem of structure and resources. 'The funding problems in relation to child abuse have been mitigated by Government money made available to the Social Services departments for this purpose following the

Cleveland report. The main problem about the staff in the neighbourhood offices being adequately trained, however, is the difficulty about releasing them for such training where that represents a cut of 20%–25% in the staff available to deal with the rest of the work.' (LJ 10.44)

2.4 MANAGING RESOURCES

Resources – both material and human – are identified as relevant to output and outcome in these child abuse inquiry cases.

Resources as the setting for the case

A distinction can be made between 'background' resources – the physical environment and its resources which are the setting for the case and resources aimed at the case. At the most poignant the Tyra Henry inquiry records 'the relative ease with which Claudette Henry was able to secure offers of housing tells a sad story. Boroughs like Lambeth first started to under finance whole blocks and estates which were decaying to the point where they could not be let even to people desperate for a home. These euphemistically are known as 'hard to let'; in reality they have become so sub-standard that people in bad housing, and even homeless people in bed and breakfast accommodation, often consider it preferable to stay where they are in the distant hope of something better than to move into a slum . . . . We draw attention to this situation because it seems to us to epitomise the unforgivable decline in human and material resources which form not only the backdrop but a main precipitant of Tyra's tragedy. Its remedy lies in more powerful hands than Lambeth's'. (TH 8.21)

The Doreen Aston inquiry heard evidence to the effect that normal conditions of the estate on which the family lived included 'high unemployment, high density of population, poor housing conditions, high and rising crime rate, drug abuse, poor take up of health services, a high level of single parenthood, and high levels of child abuse'. (DA 4.8) In the light of this the statement from the Director of Social Services for London Borough of Southwark that there had been no change in resources to the fieldwork section of the Social Services Department since 1971 was remarkable. (DA 1.22) 'It is the responsibility of senior management, local and Central government, to provide the overall resources and to determine the broad pattern of priorities for these resources, taking responsibility for decisions leading to no, or limited, services being provided.' (KC 78)

Resources aimed at the case

Resources affect alternatives being available to help the child. The inquiries are scattered with examples of this lack of resources. 'The decision to hold back from taking care proceedings did envisage providing, as an alternative, massive support. In the event massive support was never provided nor was it feasible.' (LGC 38.12 and EJH 2.4.13, 'A' 8)

The Kimberley Carlile inquiry makes that point about resources most strongly. 'Every one of the many levels in the complex organisations involved could make decisions about resources, with the decisions made at one level impinging on the others, and with levels between organisations interacting. At the head of this structure is central Government; Kimberley was at the other remote, receiving end. . . . Central Government serves children in many ways and makes various financial arrangements for their benefit. As local authorities have a major role to play in protecting children, one of the more important economic decisions made by the central government on behalf of children will be the level it provides to local authorities, especially if it accepts the onerous responsibility of setting spending targets.' (KC 65–66)

The 'A' inquiry recommended that the County Council take note of the major resource implications which will result from the Children Act 1989 and ensure that in the light of these implications it is able to fulfil its statutory duties in relation to child protection. ('A' 13)

Managing human resources

The inquiries abound with examples of problems in delivering an effective service due to staff shortages, over high work loads, and failures to provide adequate cover during periods of staff sickness or leave.

Staff shortages

'. . . the Department has failed to attract and retain sufficient numbers of experienced and qualified social workers, and this has undoubtedly added to the stresses experienced by those in post. We recognise that this is a national problem, but this of itself does not mean that Humberside should not address it.' ('A' 8) Staff shortages amplify problems of transfer of case between areas and underline the need for systems to be in place for the effective prioritisation of caseloads (for example KC 50. RF 23. DA 2.207. DA 4.23).

High turnover of staff

High turnover of staff results in discontinuity and has a profound effect on services. 'Seven health visitors were responsible for Richard's health care and development during the last five years of his life. This comparatively large number was necessitated by staff changes, and because the family moved home frequently in the early years.' (RF 108) The Kimberley Carlile inquiry noted the complete turnover of first line managers in the area team of Social Services responsible for Kimberley. (KC 75) The turnover of staff has a knock-on effect. Firstly, the recruitment of young and inexperienced staff. (RF 112) Vacancies can be left unfilled (LGC 50.1 for example). The Jasmine Beckford inquiry noted the pressure put on the area manager by the absence of senior social workers. (JB 134) The Kimberley Carlile case was managed by a team leader. And having criticised his conduct of the case and noted that there were not resource problems which effected case management the inquiry said 'We suspect that part of the problem was that he was overworked, to the detriment of his professionalism'. (KC 22)

In addition high staff turnover can have a profound effect on relationships between agencies. 'The lower the level of professional maturity in staff, the more they will need the clarity and confidence of knowing what it is they are expected to do, and seek guidance. If this situation is compounded . . . . . by high turnover of staff, unfilled vacancies, inexperience among newly promoted managers and with longer serving ones at the end of their tether, the climate becomes one of siege. This leaves some energy for routine inter-agency working, but little in terms of creative or critical development of inter-agency care plans, and the key worker could make only a limited use of the skills available in the multi disciplinary system.' (DA 5.17)

Shortages of black workers

The Liam Johnson inquiry points out the shortage of suitably qualified black workers within agencies. 'The reasons for this are outside the scope of this report. A number of those who dealt with the family were 'non-white' but the majority were. This is particularly true within the neighbourhood offices of Social Services. At the time there was only one black worker and she was part-time. Ideally they would have liked a black male worker to work with the father, particularly in the period following Liam's death. So far as we can tell, however, the father himself has never expressed the wish to have a black worker, but he may well have preferred to do so. It simply was not possible.' (LJ 1.16) Despite the fact that seven of the inquiries relate to black and minority ethnic children issues relating to the recruitment of black staff are barely touched upon despite contemporaneous encouragement by the DoH and others to take positive action.

Cover during leave and sickness

Case by case the association of avoidance by the family, and staff leave and sickness bears careful comparison. The absence of the key member of staff on leave or sickness, without adequate cover, in association with patterns of avoidance, failure to gain access, or resistance, is a warning sign in cases which should be heeded. (see below)

The availability of cover during periods of staff leave of sickness, or the availability of a worker with whom to orchestrate hand over of the case, are identified to be relevant in a number of cases. As the Liam Johnson inquiry summarises in relation to the neighbourhood office system, but with wider application 'There is no leeway within the system to provide adequate cover for absences due to sickness, leave or people being away on training'. (LJ 10.11) The social worker in the Tyra Henry case went on compassionate leave, and it was nearly three weeks before an officer could deputise for her.
(TH 3.21) Later she went on annual leave. By the time she returned 'Claudette Henry had moved with Tyra into Neil's family flat and was living there with Andrew. A fortnight later Tyra was dead.' (TH 3.21) The Emma Jane Hughes inquiry notes the sickness of the social worker and informal contact, in absence, by the senior social worker. There were no visits to the family in the month before the child's death. (EJH 2.4.67) The absence of adequate cover during periods of leave was criticised in the Aston and Woodcock inquiries. And having been on leave, without adequate cover, there are problems on return. The Richard Fraser inquiry noted that the social worker did not see Richard following his return from summer holiday although he did try to make an appointment to visit them. 'This is a serious omission, no doubt pressure of work on returning from leave must be taken into account.' (RF 69) And in the Woodcock and Carlile cases contact was broken with the family in the 'wind-up' period before a member of staff left. (SW 1.94 & KC.97)

Unallocated cases

In a variety of ways cases in these inquiries were discontinuously allocated to social workers. Only in the Kimberley Carlile case when the case was held by a team manager is the issue of unallocated cases discussed in detail. The Kimberley Carlile inquiry heard a variety of submissions concerning unallocated cases. 'We identified three categories of unallocated cases: A case where it is clear that it should be allocated, but for whatever reason, no one will accept responsibility for it; A case where it is not clear if it is going to require further work, so the decision is left until further inquiries have been made; and, A case where the nature of the work is clear, but it possesses insufficient priority to be allocated immediately; at the same time, it does not lack enough priority to prevent it being rejected immediately so it is left in suspended animation.'

'Considering the first kind of case, we can say, unequivocally, that this is not acceptable with a child abuse case. Concerning the second category, we believe that it has two potential dangers: first, ambiguity might exist concerning accountability for the case while it is unallocated, with the likelihood that the team manager will be left literally holding the baby; and second, there is a risk that an unallocated case will drift into oblivion . . . a definite plan must be made, to be completed within a specified time scale and with clear accountability. The last category might be appropriate if there is a reasonable assumption that better times lie ahead. We would be worried, however, if it is used as a way of avoiding hard decisions and of disguising lack of resources, or if it is used as a method of pretending that an office can do more than its resources actually permit.' The inquiry recommended that any Social Services Department accommodation of unallocated cases must establish the appropriate criteria whenever a case remains unallocated, and policies to determine what happens next, including a clear definition of accountability for each case. (KC 75–77) The recently redefined role of the key worker as case co-ordinator could permit unallocated cases to be disguised, and services fail to be provided that, other things being equal, should be.

The Carlile and Beckford inquiries say that 'resources were available in this case . . . . .' (KC 65) and 'we do not consider that shortage of resources was a significant factor in this case, saving respect of the continuing deficiency of senior social workers in Area 6'. (JB 134) These inquiries underestimate the consequences, in each case, of the worker who had face to face contact with the family, also acting in a managerial role because of lack of available staff resources.

Administrative and clerical support

A substantial number of inquiries refer to inadequate administrative and clerical support, (for example SW 3.17, JB 134, KC 73). Administrative staffing levels being low can prevent the maintenance of details of accurate records (LGP 6.15), and the absence of adequate departmental administrative procedures. (SW 3.17) 'The fundamental problem is that whenever there are financial constraints administrative staff tend to be regarded as expendable. It seems to us that at the very least the system whereby each social work team had a clerk who knew the work and was able to deal with the routine tasks ought to be reinstated as soon as possible.' (LJ 10.19) As a consequence inquiries note that health visitor and social work staff spend 'unreasonable portions on their time on work of a clerical nature'. (DA 4.31 & EJH 5.4)

Lack of facilities

In addition inquiries note the poverty of physical resources – the facilities – in which administrative and professional staff have to work. 'The waiting area is public. The interview rooms have glass windows and adjoin the waiting area. The room which was intended to be the focal point of community activities is too small for many of them to be held there and is in any event the only available space for conferences, supervising access, staff supervision and almost any activity which can't be carried out at a desk. . . . It seems to us that this environment certainly does not encourage a nervous woman, or perhaps the neighbour of an abused child, to unburden themselves' (LJ 10.9 to 10.26 also for example KC 110.73).

2.5 THE MANAGEMENT OF STAFF CARE

The Cleveland report addresses the question of stress in relation to effectiveness. 'There was a common acknowledgement of the heavy emotional demands and profound impact this area of work (sexual abuse) has on professionals. Of universal concern was the way in which, if staff are inadequately supported or lack special training, they can quickly lose confidence and become overwhelmed by the complexity of the problems they are seeking to resolve.' (CLV 13.34)

But, as the Doreen Aston inquiry records, it is not necessarily the specific stress caused by the family, or threats of violence, that can have cumulative impact on professional workers: 'The panel had evidence that the area was difficult and potentially violent. The crime rate impinged on staff and the panel were told that on more than one occasion staff had been mugged whilst carrying out their duties. These factors no doubt added another stressful component for managers and staff working in an already stressful environment. The effects of stress on staff should not be underestimated'. (DA 4.11)

The burden of stress on professional workers should not be underestimated and requires that managers develop staff care strategies. The Kimberley Carlile inquiry considers violence and stress in social work noting that four social workers had died in the course of their work in the previous three years. It quotes a statement made by the Association of Directors of Social Services that 'the safety of employees . . . is a management responsibility. Managers must structure policies, procedures and back up support in such a manner that they are not influenced primarily by resource availability, but rather by their effectiveness'. The inquiry notes that the employee has a responsibility too, especially in identifying situations where violence or risk of such is a potential problem, and in identifying any particular areas where they have problems of their own connected with violence. (KC 196)

Conclusion

This section has attempted to bring together matters relating to the organisational context of professional practice in child abuse cases. This form of analysis may understate the feeling gained from some of the inquiries, especially those of the late 80s (KC. DA. and LJ), of the condition in which professionals, especially social workers and health visitors are working: the social deprivation and potential violence they face, the heavy workloads, and continual problems of resources. The inquiries describe the increased level of reporting of child abuse cases, but this is only one aspect of the work of these agencies. There are many competing demands for resources which are available. As financial constraint continues and the Children Act 1989 and community care legislation are implemented, what kind of service to abused children and their families, can and will, be provided? Lack of resources should not be seen as an 'addendum' to the problems associated with preventing child death, nor is it acceptable as an excuse. Adequate resources are central and crucial to the provision of an effective child care service.

SECTION 3 INTER-AGENCY WORKING

This section looks at what the inquiries have said about the key elements of the inter-agency system: the case conference; the role of the key worker; the child abuse/child protection register; and the role of the ACPC.

A lesson to be learned from the 1980s is that inter-agency working is not easy, and not self evidently useful. That is not to say that an individual agency can go it alone, but separate viewpoints and confusion of roles, as well as the availability of multiple pathways for communication, are a recipe for muddle. This is especially so when two sets of rules are operating – the law and 'child abuse procedures'. There must be clarity about how they relate. The framework of relationships regulated by the area child protection committee must be energetically and strategically planned.

3.1 SEPARATE VIEWPOINTS?

The previous synthesis of child abuse inquiries identified duplicated functions as an issue of concern, particularly between NSPCC and Social Services Departments. A far stronger theme in the 80s has been the problem of separate viewpoints.

The inquiries focus on several reasons for separate viewpoints, including a clash of personalities (JB 108), and gender and status, for example female day care workers, health visitors and teachers feeling that their views were not taken sufficiently seriously. (RF 72) Then there were differences within the social work profession about how to act in pursuit of the 'best interest of the child' (LGC 35.11), and within the medical profession, about the way to diagnose child sexual abuse. There were misunderstandings of roles between professionals (CLV 18 and 3.19) These separations of viewpoint between professionals are compounded by turnovers of staff. (LGC 1)

Pressure of time and resources affects communication. 'When colleagues are all hard pressed, the amount of effort required to contact them before communication is achieved can be frustrating and time consuming, and when administrative or clerical support is unavailable, the good practice of confirming issues of decisions by letter is difficult to sustain. There are differing views between agencies about the extent to which talking about families (clients) as well as directly with them is integral to the work and therefore valuable and legitimate professional activity.' (DA 5.17)

There was concern about 'shifts in emphasis which appeared to occur between verbal and written communication between workers and different disciplines. This was evident from comparing the running records of phone calls between social workers and health visitors, with the significance and implications of facts observed by health visitors not being recognised sufficiently. The receiver of the information needs to know WHY it is important'. (DA 5.18)

Selective disclosure of information by agencies to one another may be inadequate. 'There is no problem about this in the obvious and serious cases. No one fails to disclose having seen serious injuries to a child but there are . . . . . very real tensions between the functions of the agencies in relation to child protection and their more usual roles.' (LJ 6.33–34)

A consequence of separate viewpoints is that agencies have unrealistic expectations of other agencies powers on what they are able to achieve. 'It is commonly assumed that if a person has convictions, the police 'will know', there might be expectation that health visitors will 'keep an eye on things'. (LJ 6.16–17) (The) question of each agency's powers, procedures and what they can or cannot do is a matter for urgent interagency training and information.' (LJ 6.21)

Many of the inquiries show concern about misperceptions of role and responsibility between professionals trying to work together. (CLV 2.43, LGP 6.12, CP 7.3) They see the need for development of mutual trust in working together and passing information. (JC 3.2.2 and LJ 7.2.2) The need for personal contact between workers jointly involved with families cannot be overstated. (CP 7.3)

At the heart of the question of separate viewpoints, is the question of the nature and shared understanding of the statutory responsibilities of child protection agencies.

The Reuben Carthy inquiry expresses concern that whereas health visitors and social workers were required to refer the matter to the statutory agency with the power and duty to ensure that action is taken to protect the child, that is the Social Services Department, other professional colleagues within the multi-agency framework were not required to. The inquiry considered that this element of discretion was unsatisfactory. It felt that health visitors and social workers 'are entitled to conduct their own responsibilities in the expectation that other professionals in the possession of such information have an identical obligation to act under the procedures'. (RC 141–3)

It is the Social Services Department which carries the prime responsibility for the protection of children at risk. The Liam Johnson inquiry rightly draws attention to the confusion between 'child abuse procedures' in relation to the law. 'Working Together' states that 'the primary responsibility to Social Services Department does not diminish the role of other agencies or the need for inter-agency co-operation in the planning and providing of services for a child or family'. Whilst in many cases there is no obvious inconsistency the Liam Johnson inquiry highlighted the problems that can arise where there is. (LJ 8.2)

'A fundamental issue which has not been resolved is whether the role of other agencies is to supply the Social Services Department with the relevant information in their possession to enable the department to carry out its statutory function of protecting children, or whether they are all genuinely co-operating fully and equally in the child's interests regardless of the legitimate need of their own agencies. All the difficulties which we outline stem from this fundamental, unresolved issue.' (LJ 7.2)

Misunderstandings may arise if a paediatrician, does not understand the social workers statutory duty to protect that child when a firm and unequivocal diagnosis of serious sexual abuse is made (CLV 8.8.74), or may result from a paediatrician not appreciating the difficulty in which equivocation places statutory authorities. (KMcG 16) Paediatricians may develop unrealistic expectations of Social Services powers 'and take a view that however important the other agencies may be when it comes to dealing with the family, Social Services ought to do something'. (LJ 6.16)

What is clear is that whilst the statutory responsibility for child protection may lie with Social Services, 'health and environment are inseparable components for child's well-being, and therefore doctors also share a responsibility for the wider care and protection of their child patients'. (LGP 5.34) The Carlile inquiry considers it bad practice for any of the other agencies to assume that, the duty to investigate cases of child abuse, or decisions on actions pursuing to those duties can be left to Social Services. It considers that health service personnel must in future acknowledge and accept involvement in intervention. This may be particularly appropriate when what is needed most urgently is the medical examination of the unseen child. (KC 127–129)

The 'duty of care' of agencies other than the Social Services Department needs much clearer definition.

3.2 CASE CONFERENCES (see also 4.5 Intervention and Planning)

A number of inquiries refer to simple but important discrepancies between ACPC and departmental procedure manuals. (HK 6.9) Confusion may be compounded when the ACPC manual, rather the department manual is the first point of reference, especially for Social Services staff. (LJ 8.6) The 'case conference' may complicate this further. Some inquiries are clear that the case conference makes recommendations and that the Social Services Departments make decisions. (CS 17 and 9, DA 8.11, DH 6.18) The inquiries themselves discuss case conferences at length, without fully addressing the decision making processes within individual agencies or the importance of continuity of the planning processes within the agencies.

Confusion about the role of case conferences by Social Services staff is described. The team leader in the Doreen Aston case deferred action until a case conference had been held, during which time the child died. The inquiry recommends that the Social Services Department should not refrain from taking necessary action because a case conference is imminent. The case conferences should not be used by other agencies as a substitute for taking action which probably belongs to themselves.

The Tyra Henry inquiry expresses a deeper concern that the local authority used the NAI review to fulfil the function of the statutory care review, a formulation which prioritises the non statutory function. The inquiry considered that this contributed to a repeated failure to address key issues about the child's long term safety and to question whether the local authority was taking proper care of her. ' . . . It is the known possibility of ill-treatment which gives the local authority its duty to seek, and a court its power to make, a care order. Registering and monitoring a child as at risk of non accidental injury is a secondary use of the same information, principally to ensure that a multidisciplinary watch is kept.' We consider that there is a substantial danger that the NAI procedure will dominate the case conference if it is allowed to do so and will swing the discussion away from the in-depth planning for the child's future towards a short-term and often superficial consideration of the child's current physical 'well-being'. (TH 6.12)

The inquiries of the 80s emphasise particular purposes of case conferences and pitfalls. A significant problem can be 'the lack of understanding of the main purpose of the case conferences and the nature of decisions which could or had been taken'. The crucial purpose, according to an unpublished report and the Beckford inquiry is to recommend actions which should be taken by those who are legally responsible for action to further the welfare of the child. (JB 251 also LJP 6.6)

The clear formulation that a purpose of a case conference is to provide information to assist the local authority in the discharge of its statutory responsibilities, would be helpful. Rule frameworks for decision making within the local authority need to be as clear as the purposes of case conferences.

Clarity about the authority of the individual agency vis a vis the corporacy of the case conference group is essential. The Aston inquiry describes clearly the purpose of case conferences is to plan. And it seeks to clarify the authority of the corporate decision as follows: 'whilst individual agencies are responsible for implementing a plan, any deviation from it should only be made, except in emergencies, after prior consultation with the key worker with the other agencies. The conference is only the opportunity where all come together and can see and hear and discuss in detail'. (DA 6.2)

There are inherent dangers: 'Dissent from common policies may be explicitly or implicitly discouraged; . . . case conference minutes may mislead those not present at the meeting unless they have been carefully prepared and checked by all in attendance. It is essential that the status of recommendations and conclusions should be clarified in the minutes'. (LGP 6.9)

The McGoldrick inquiry notes that the 'very act of sharing concern can sometimes dissipate that concern' (KMcG 60) but that view is perilously close to the view that 'if you can't think of what else to do have a case conference'. (LJ 8.28) Dissipation of concern clearly can only follow establishing the problem, and formulating the plan. Child abuse registration, about which it is one purpose of the case conference to decide, should not provide a false sense of security and is not an end in itself (see below).

The Beckford inquiry among others, is sceptical about the degree of objectivity which case conferences afford decision making. Bringing together a mixture of professional disciplines may not achieve a desired objectivity; indeed the larger the spread of disciplines more unwieldy the case conference is likely to be and more muffled will be the message to Social Services. (JB 250–1)

The inquiries, variously, distinguish child abuse case conferences from other forms of meetings. But there is not agreement between them. For example, the Tyra Henry inquiry makes a telling differentiation between child abuse case conferences, and statutory reviews of children in care. (TH 6.15) The 'A' inquiry describes informal in-house meeting as 'case discussions' but describes, 'case conference' as a term reserved for a formal multi-disciplinary meeting to make decisions about a child in care. ('A' 9) This notably fits the model of the Tyra Henry inquiry which would subordinate the child abuse case conferences to statutory case reviews in respect of children who are both subject to a statutory order, and on the child abuse register. (See also LJ 3.87–88 and CS 18)

What is clear is that the purpose of all meetings must be understood by all concerned, and so must the relationship of all meetings to the purposes and tasks of the initial child abuse case conference.

When to call the initial case conference

If the concern is that a child may be abused or neglected then the formality of a child abuse case conference in which information is shared, is essential. Clearly fine judgement is needed. On the one hand, calling a formal conference may be a fail-safe; on the other the multi-disciplinary case conference should be used sparingly. (LGC 67.7)

There is consensus that a child abuse case conference should be called after a reported incidence of child abuse, but disagreement about the timing. The Doreen Aston inquiry takes the view that 'there is a need for a degree of professional flexibility in this respect'. It expresses concern that very tight deadlines on conferences – within 48 hours – are unrealistic and argues that procedures should recognise the reality. (DA 6.5) Inquiries express a view that case conferences should be convened at a point before the final court hearing, and after the court hearing to assist the local authority to plan how to discharge its statutory responsibilities, not least on the basis of new information gained during the court process (JB 89 & an unpublished report), and before placement. (SW. JB. CH.) In addition, pre birth. (DA 4.2)

Who should attend case conferences

Parent and child attendance at case conferences is commented upon in the Beckford and Cleveland reports. (JB 249) The Cleveland report recommended that 'parents should be informed of case conferences and invited to attend for all or part of the conference unless, in the view of the chairman of the conference, their presence will preclude a full and proper consideration of the child's interests'. (CLV 246) The Liam Johnson inquiry noted the problem of parents attending when matters relating to prosecutions was under discussion. The Cleveland inquiry recommends 'irrespective of whether parents attend the conferences, social workers owe a primary responsibility to ensure that the case conference has information relating to the family background and the parents as opposed to reviews on the issues under consideration'. (CLV 246)

The Beckford inquiry alone considers that matter of child attendance at case conferences and takes the view that 'the answer must lie with the child. The child must be asked whether he wishes to be involved in a case conference . . . If a child should opt not to attend, then we consider it of paramount importance to have his views canvassed and represented at such conference. In order to obtain the views of the child himself, rather than those relayed by the social worker in the case, it might be appropriate to use a person of the child's own choosing, who canvasses the wishes of the child and ultimately passes them on to the case conference members'. (JB 250) 'Whatever decision is made concerning the child's attendance, the person chairing the conference should, as a matter of standard practice, consider the issue of whether the child should be involved or not.' (JB 250)

Attendance of foster parents

The Beckford inquiry is cautious about the attendance of foster parents at case conferences 'The division of view focused on the issue of confidentiality'. While all our witnesses favoured the attendance of foster parents in principle, it was felt that their presence at case conferences 'could seriously inhibit professional people who would be willing to reveal confidences, but not if non-professionals are present. We see the force of this objection. Once foster parents have considerable experience of rearing and nurturing the child, then it should be possible to accommodate their presence at case conferences, at the very least part of it.' (JB 249)

Attendance of professionals

In relation to the attendance of professionals, a balance needs to be struck between obtaining the attendance of those who have something to say, and holding the case conference within a reasonable period of time. The McGoldrick inquiry considers that if key personnel are unable to attend the chairman should consider delaying the case conference to allow optimal attendance. (KMcG 75) A number of inquiries emphasise the need to obtain the attendance of general practitioners at case conferences. The GPs should invariably be invited. (JB 245) Inquiries emphasise the role of the school representative at a case conference, it being the matter of debate whether the best person is the head teacher or the class teacher. The Beckford inquiry takes the view that the designated officer would clearly be the most appropriate person. (JB 245)

Inquiries emphasise the need for legal advice at case conferences (CLV 247 for example), though the Aston inquiry extends a word of caution should this replace direct communication between the solicitor and those responsible for giving the solicitor instructions. (DA.6.44)

Case conferences about transfer of cases

The Aston inquiry also emphasises that when a case is to be transferred a representative of the receiving authority having been warned or having had a chance to respond or be present at the conference. (DA 6.47)

Continuity of attendance

The Jason Caesar inquiry considered that each case conference subsequent to the initial one should formally review the need to involve staff in agencies not currently represented at the case conference (JC 3.4.23), and the Gates inquiry noted lack of continuity of attendance at conferences (LGC 18.1) which needs to be taken account particularly in the manner of obtaining information from the new representative, ensuring accurate recording in minutes and ensuring continuity in how the case is perceived and dealt with.

Exchange of information

Conventions around confidentiality need to be clarified nationally, and locally. Confidentiality is still regarded as a barrier to full communication less now in relation to the medical profession, than the police. (LJ. DA) A number of inquiries recommend that written information is circulated beforehand, so that an opportunity is provided to check accuracy and confirm interpretations.

Case history

The Doreen Aston inquiry recommends that not only should written information be provided to the case conference about the observations of individual workers but that every social worker allocated to a child abuse case should be required to produce a written case history for an initial case conference, to be updated for later review case conferences, and to produce a child protection plan for discussion at the case conference or as soon as possible thereafter if it is held in an emergency. (DA 6.35–40 & DA 6.27) An unpublished report suggests that in addition to circulation of information beforehand, there should be a common agenda for all conferences throughout the authority achieved by check list for the chair, and the agenda and the purpose of the conference to be set out with the invitation.

Fact and opinion

There is a need for all participants of case conferences to distinguish fact from opinion in their presentations to the conference. An unpublished report makes a telling point that some of the participants in a case conference had very little legitimate basis on which to offer opinions, and the credibility of some of those opinions might be open to question where there was a more rigorous examination of the decision making process that took place at the time.

Communication within conferences

A number of inquiries make the point that everyone in a case conference should be given the opportunity, and be able, to express a point of view. (RF 120 also LGC 5.14, KMcG 37 & 60, & JB 82)

Problems of communication are most telling if they appear to be related to occupational status. Commenting on the disregarding of the health visitor information the Beckford inquiry says 'we cannot help feeling that throughout our inquiry the worth and the status of health visitors are not always given the credit they deserve'. (JB 82) And also in the Cleveland inquiry 'social workers did not regard themselves as competent to question the basis of the medical diagnosis from a consultant paediatrician whom they treated with respect due to that status'. (CLV 4.189)

Accurate minutes, fully distributed and properly corrected

There are examples of confusion around the status of recommendations when the case conferences have been inaccurately minuted (EJH 2.4.3 & RF 120 for example). In the Richard Fraser case one of the decisions simply read 'low profile visiting (as in above summary)'. That 'summary' defined 'low profile visiting' as 'routine visits'. (RF 120)

Procedures should specify that all professional participants receive copies of all written reports (CS 17) and the minutes must be fully distributed. (DA 6.22 also KMcG 77) Accurate minutes properly circulated are an essential part of case management providing a basis for clarity of planning and clarity of review.

The Aston inquiry has some useful comments on the minuting of case conferences. 'It is essential that minutes set out recommendations and reasons on which they are based . . . Narrative may be helpful in sharing information but need not usually be minuted. The minutes should provide a succinct record of the discussion, highlighting the information and processes that led to the recommendations recorded, and clearly indicating who was responsible for future actions . . . . .' (DA 6.17–21) 'Finally, minutes must be corrected.' (TH 6.23, LGC 47.5 & RF 120)

Chairing case conferences

The inquires lay heavy emphasis on the crucial role of the chair of the case conference. 'Chairing case conferences is patently a skilled and time consuming job. We can only reiterate recommendations of previous reports that local authorities should develop systems for ensuring that case conferences are chaired competently by an independent manager, who has been trained for the task' (DA 6.15 also TH 6.18 for example).

Six points can be made about the chair's role, in summary. Firstly the chair should provide a leadership role ensuring that the interests of the child remain paramount amongst the discussions. (KMcG 76) Secondly, the chair should ensure that all the members of the conference are allowed sufficient time and opportunity to present their information and opinions. (KMcG 76) Thirdly, the chairman should be challenging and probing. 'Our underlying view is that supervision and chairing are the specific, empirical points in the management of a case . . . . . and that a multiplication of paper procedures, for example by reviewing all minutes, is a fallible and bureaucratic second best.' (TH 7.15 also LGP 5.93)

This role leads to a fourth point, that the need for incisive and decisive chairing is constricted by closeness of the chair to the key personnel at the conference. 'The dominance of the NAI aspect exacerbated this problem in Tyra's case, for it is here that the risk of collusion is sharpest and most damaging to good decision-making . . . . . We consider that the chairing is so important in this field and a possible result of inadequate chairing so grave that it needs to be made a rule that no case conference may be chaired by a person who has line management responsibility for the non-accidental injury aspect of the case.' (TH 6.19)

Fifthly the chair has a responsibility for ensuring that a protection plan is formulated and long and short term aims established. The chair should ensure that everyone is clear about who has responsibility for the implementation of the plans, and when, and in what circumstances the case conference should be reconvened. (DA 6.14) Finally the chair is the focal point for the circulation of written information before and after the case conference and is in a central point of contact, along with the key worker, in a continuous process of planning and review.

3.3 KEY WORKER ROLE

The key workers role has evolved over the years. 'Working Together' describes the role as a focal point for the co-ordination and communication about the case. 'The key worker should not only be well known to others participating in the case, but should have a good and close relationship with them. By his own actions, he should inspire confidence in his co-ordinating leadership.' (RF 126–127) A similar point is made by the Aston inquiry. 'Key workers carry heavy responsibilities and are perceived by workers in other agencies as the person who ought to have a grip on the issues and be pursuing them actively and effectively.' (DA 5.14–15)

The example of the Aston case suggests that care should be taken over the role of key worker as co-ordinator rather than as an active case worker. The establishment of the role as co-ordinator, only, must be based on sound case work judgement. She did not feel, and was not perceived by others to be, effective. (DA 5.15)

The Beckford inquiry summarises the additional role for the front line social worker when she is also the key worker as being a role which: notifies all the professionals involved in the case of her own position as a key worker and tells them how to contact her; records promptly and files all written communications; disseminates all sorts of information promptly to the relevant professionals; keeps under review the involvement of other agencies concerned with the family; actively seeks information from other professionals. (JB 219)

3.4 CHILD PROTECTION REGISTERS

The Lucy Gates panel inquiry says 'We share in the scepticism expressed by many of our colleagues about the value of child abuse registers because there is confusion over the purpose of registers; there is confusion as to which children should be on them and which should not; when their names should be added and when they should be removed; they can create a false sense of security; it may be assumed that only those children on the register needed attention; at what point do all children need to be kept under surveillance if the number of children who harm children increases? However, as long as the official child abuse register system exists, it is essential that every practical step is taken to follow the agreed procedure. Registers become pointless if professionals do not make use of them or if there are difficulties in obtaining access such as outside normal office hours'. (LGP 6.5)

Government guidelines, 'Working Together', clarify that the primary purpose of child protection registers is to provide a focus for inter-agency planning and every child on the register is expected to have a protection plan. The McGoldrick inquiry considers that 'Although it is now much less likely that a child with a series of injuries which lead to suspicion of child abuse could pass through the case conference without registration, this is still possible if members of the case conference have a particular set of beliefs and judgements which fail to recognise the significance of the injuries. We would therefore like to see a statement in the section of the Child Protection Handbook On Registration that the primary function of registration is to protect the interests of the child. Registration should include all children who have been abused, those who are at risk of future abuse, those who need an inter'agency plan of supervision and treatment and those children and families where regular inter-agency reviews are considered necessary'. (KMcG 78)

Inquiries consider whether or not registration, non registration, or deregistration made any difference to the outcome of the case. The McGoldrick inquiry is clear that decisions not to register had a detrimental effect on the handling and perception of the case by those concerned and in all probability on the outcome. (KMcG 60) 'We feel that registration would have heightened further the levels of awareness and concern of those involved (the decision not to register was in itself a positive one) and registration would have ensured a formal review of the case after the third case conference.' (KMcG 59) The Beckford inquiry says that 'Once the Beckford children were taken off the child abuse register in 1982 it was inevitable that the input of social work would substantially reduce. And so it was'. In that case deregistration was a reflection of the view of, and plan for, the case of the team leader and social worker. Discussion at the point of consideration of deregistration could have elicited this. (JB 120).

A number of inquiries offer views about registration procedure and the need to keep the register up to date. (JB 32, CH 3.7, LGC 44.10) The inquiries do not discuss appropriate criteria for deregistration.

The Tyra Henry inquiry suggests that the unborn second child should have been registered as at risk of non accidental injury at the maternity hospital and local clinics be warned to be particularly alert to any signs of physical abuse at check ups or an admission. (TH 2.32) This view fits well to the Aston proposals for pre-birth conferences, and is covered by recent Government guidance.

The Liam Johnson inquiry was extremely concerned that there was a period of a few months when the register was unable to be kept up to date because of lack of adequate administrative support. 'The accurate maintenance of the register is essentially an administrative task. A register which is not accurate and up to date, in our view is worse than useless. If the child's name should be on it and is not, it is likely to give a false sense of security to someone from another agency.' (LJ 8.25) Implicit in this view, and also views expressed in the early 80s by the Lucy Gates inquiry (LJC 44.10) is a view of registers as useful in providing information to assist the immediate protection of children, as well as long term planning. This view is not reflected in Government guidelines.

Three inquiries expressed concern about multiple registers operating within local authority or health authority areas or 'two tier' systems of registration. 'Whilst we think such systems are useful tools, it is essential that they do not become mini child protection registers.' (LJ 8.24, LGC 31.5 & KMcG 28–29)

The Aston and Johnson inquiries offer final reflections on child protection registers '(Doreen) was on the child abuse register, everyone concerned knew that and in large part followed the procedures established for a child on the register. Let it not be thought therefore that the child protection register (as named in 'Working Together' page 25) can itself protect a child. It may create a dangerous complacency to think of it as more than a record of registered children for whom plans have to be made and reviewed'. (DA 8.6) And, 'Placing a child's name on the register is not a magic spell which thereafter protects the child from evil. It is a way of alerting professionals to the fact that a child is thought to be at risk'. (LJ 3.93).

3.5 THE CHILD ABUSE CO-ORDINATOR

A noteworthy point in itself is that in only one case did the child abuse co-ordinator figure significantly in the sequence of events. That was the Kimberley Carlile case which reflected upon the role accordingly. 'One of the principle functions of a child abuse co-ordinator is to act as consultant to individual practitioners carrying child abuse cases. A consultant should never seek to supplant the supervisor, but should supplement supervision by providing specialist advice and guidance based on the perception and analysis of the case by the person seeking consultation. It is the function of the consultant to probe the inquirer and to make sure that all the relevant information is retrieved from the files in order that proper advice and guidance can be given.' The inquiry was concerned that the consultant mainly endorsed and was not probing enough, and criticises the manner of its initiation and that it took place over the telephone. No face to face meeting was undertaken and the file was not available for reference. (KC 119)

The Liam Johnson inquiry considers problems relating the role of child abuse co-ordinator. 'They can easily get sucked into attending case conferences, or as we have seen, into administrative tasks associated with their role, and have less and less time to a real resource for the neighbourhood offices in terms of expertise and advice.'
(LJ 10.39–42 also JB 131 and JC 3.2.3)

3.6 INTER-AGENCY PROCEDURES: ACTION FOR THE FUTURE?

The Cleveland inquiry makes a number of practical recommendations to promote inter-agency co-operation, doubtless choosing the work in 'inter-agency' rather than 'multi-disciplinary' deliberately to emphasise whole organisations working together rather than simply a sharing of professional skills. It recommends the development of inter-agency co-operation which acknowledges:

i. no single agency – health, Social Services, police or voluntary organisation has the pre-eminent responsibility in the assessment of child abuse generally and child sexual abuse specifically. Each agency has a prime responsibility for a particular aspect of the problem. Neither children's nor parents' needs and rights can be adequately met or protected unless agencies agree a framework for their inter-action. The statutory duties of Social Service Departments must be recognised;

ii. careful consideration must be given to the detail or working arrangements between doctors, nurses, social workers, police, teachers, staff of voluntary organisations and others responsible for the care of the children;

iii. arrangements for collaboration between services must not inhibit prompt action by any professional or agency where this is demanded by the best interests of the child. Agreements over collaborative work should not inhibit or preclude doctors, social workers, policemen from carrying out their primary professional responsibilities. The responsibility for the decisions will remain theirs;

iv. practical issues need to be recognised and resolved at local level in careful discussion between the respective agencies;

v. managers should accept responsibility for ensuring that agreements reached are implemented in practice. Each agency should give an undertaking not to make unilateral changes in practice or policy without giving prior notice to the others;

vi. the existence of bodies charged with the responsibility to co-ordinate practice between agencies does not relieve chief officers such as the Director of Social Services, the Chief Constable, the Director of Education and the Health Service District General Manager of their responsibility to ensure effective co-operation and collaboration between their services or to identify problems and seek solutions.' (CLV 248)

The emphasis in the set of proposals is on statutory responsibilities with co-operation to discharge these. The implications of this formation for the way agencies advise and assist the Social Services Departments, the nature of their duties of care, and for the appropriate relationship between inter-agency child abuse procedures and the law, await further debate.

The role of the Area Child Protection Committee

Problems relating to the role of the Area Child Protection Committee are identified. 'The agency representatives on the ACPC . . . all hold relatively senior posts, often a specialist child abuse post, within their agency . . . . The difficulty is that more than a year after 'Working Together' the ACPC has no budget, no delegated responsibilities, no secretariat and what it is actually able to achieve is extremely limited. It is not unique in this, so far as we are aware there is no ACPC in the country which has established a joint budget . . . It has been difficult for us to establish precisely what the ACPC has done.' (LJ 9.1–9.4)

The Cleveland inquiry related the performance of the ACPC to the handling of cases! The Area Review Committee and the Joint Child Abuse Committee provided for the most part an ineffective mechanism to co-ordinate the work of the key agencies in the field of child sexual abuse. Having successfully established guidelines for the co-ordination of physical abuse, the committee had difficulty in defining its future role and function in isolation from its constituent agencies. Representatives attending may have more consent to protect what they saw as departmental interests than to commit themselves to a prime purpose of establishing an effective co-ordinating mechanism'. (CLV 3.59–65)

'We are left with an overwhelming impression of a talking shop in which there is a good level of rapport and co-operation between the individuals who comprise the ACPC and its sub-committees, but the agencies whom they represent continue largely to perform their task in ignorance of these deliberations and achievements.' (LJ 9.4)

The Cleveland inquiry is clear that 'to be effective, the Committee needed its purpose to be defined and agreed between the chief officers and senior managers of participating agencies'. (CLV 3.67) The Cleveland report describes how when senior managers are not in agreement and not in touch, the ACPC does not offer an effective forum for co-ordinating child protection work. Inquiries offer different views about how this should be resolved, and what the role of the ACPC should be.

Representation

The chairmanship should be held by a person of calibre, sufficiently experienced in both perhaps the policy issues to ensure that problems are properly conceived and resolved. (CLV 3.69)

The Cleveland inquiry is clear that the membership of these committees should include those who have the authority and responsibility to bind their agency to implementing the recommendations of the Committee, and to play a useful part in the decision-making process which accurately reflects the view of the agency they represent. (CLV 248)

Each agency needs to have formulated the basic principles and framework of its own practice and be committed to the importance of co-ordinating work with others. (CLV 3.67)

The Aston inquiry noted that general factors which were likely to have effected the successful working of the ARC were the different levels of agency representatives, the variable attendances of some representatives, and when substitutes were nominated to attend on behalf of the agency, the thoroughness with which they had been briefed. (DA 5.6) The Johnson inquiry noted the extent to which individuals on the ACPC are empowered to bind the agency varies. (LJ 9.10) And the Cleveland inquiry adds that the role and function of any subgroup or of any working party needs to be properly defined and authorised, serves to ensure that the prime role and purpose of the co-ordinating committee is not dissipated. (CLV 3.68)

Funding

The effectiveness of ACPCs depends on member agencies resourcing them adequately. Resources are needed to give administrative support to committee work and disseminating information, and to assist in the course of multi-disciplinary training. Because inter-agency co-operation is costly in resource terms, agencies need to feel that the investment of staff time and energy brings an improved level of protection of the children at risk. (DA 5.11 also KC 162)

The need for clarity of role

If the ACPC is ever going to be effective, there needs to be a clear agreement with the individual agencies about which matters are properly the concern of the ACPC over which it should have control. (LJ 9.7).

Some proposals for the role of the ACPC would seem to pitch it into headlong confusion with the responsibilities of individual agencies. For example the Koseda inquiry suggests that 'the ACPC must be satisfied that all agencies undertaking child abuse work in its area have adequate resources to provide qualified staff, continuity, administrative backup, and effective management and supervision'. 'We endorse the recommendation of the (NSPCC's) management review that 'where an effective service cannot be provided, work limitation and/or the closure of the facility be introduced.' (HK 2.32 also 6.9) The Reuben Carthy inquiry was 'strongly of the opinion that the Area Review Committee has a clear responsibility to decide what action should be taken by the various professionals involved with child welfare in circumstances in which child abuse is identified and a duty to ensure that procedures which the Committee sets up co-ordinate the expected action to be taken in an unambiguous framework'. (RC 145) Both the Heidi Koseda and Reuben Carthy inquiries consisted of ARC representatives.

Reviewing and updating inter-agency procedures

The Aston inquiry makes the point that although the ACPC lacks the authority to take up with member agencies strategic issues about resource allocation and service delivery 'It could however, have reviewed, for example, cross-borough working in practice so as to satisfy itself that mutual understandings between agencies were sufficiently clear and capable of being implemented'. (DA 5.3)

Inquiries endorse the need for the Committee to establish, maintain and review common procedures, and emphasise the need for these to be made available through effective distribution of a procedures handbook. (LGP 5.33, CP 7.5, HK 6.8, KC.162)

The Aston inquiry makes the useful point that local guidelines of child abuse should be no more than two documents for any individual worker to read. (DA 6.4) Clearly, it is a matter for individual agencies to sort out the relationship between their child abuse procedures and their procedures relating to other aspects of child care work.

The Liam Johnson inquiry, rightly, thinks that the ACPC should look at the essential nature of inter-agency co-operation. As a one off response to a child abuse inquiry, it is important. However, there is a wider need for such a review. Even if this was periodic, perhaps as part of an annual review process, it would allow the essential nature of relationships, particularly in relation to statutory responsibilities, to be reviewed against developments in agency strategy and resources,and professional practice (LJ 9.8–9).

Monitoring

Inquiries note the role for ACPCs in monitoring practice in individual cases. The Aston inquiry recommends that ACPCs should include in their tasks the periodic review of the work of case conferences. (DA 5.2)

Training

Inquiries endorse the co-ordination of training role of ACPCs, as described above. In addition the Reuben Carthy inquiry recommends that the ARC 'examines urgently the need for a co-ordinated programme of publicity to ensure that the community is aware of the need to act in cases in which children are known or suspected to be the victims of abuse, the publicity to make clear to the community the services available from the welfare agencies to receive referral concerning abuse'. (RC 36)

Inquiries

This role is reflected upon in a number of inquiries (JB 239, DA 5.11 & LJ 16.4 for example). It is commented upon in the Conclusion (below) and will be the subject or revised DoH guidelines.

The future

The Kimberley Carlile inquiry concluded that 'the time is right for a choice between a single agency as provider of child protection service and a thorough-going shared responsibility'. (KC 29) The former option could be achieved either through establishing one statutory child protection authority employing all relevant staff and doing all the work, or by assigning to one authority the overall responsibility for the child protection service and giving it power for this purpose to require the assistance of professionals working in other agencies. Given that the first model is probably too radical to gain support, the inquiry concentrates on the second. It notes advantages and disadvantages – accountability would be clear but the contributions from other agencies could be marginalised. A multi-disciplinary responsibility has the disadvantage of inducing ambiguity of accountability.

'We think that it is unclear what kind of child protection service society wants. We seem, in many ways, to have travelled far down the road towards a shared, multi-disciplinary responsibility, while retaining features of the one authority system, with Social Services Departments the primary, although not exclusive authority for the entire system. . . . . . Indeed any managerial responsibility for the system is usually absent, with the brunt of the criticism borne by individual practitioners, often low in the employment hierarchy, as if they acted as independent professionals. If this analysis is accurate, one should not be surprised if it is remarkably difficult to bring lasting improvements to the system.' (KC 140–141) It notes that the same flaws in the system have been repeatedly exposed by various child abuse inquiries. It considers that 'the child protection system as a whole is less than the aggregate of its several parts. It is a puppet with no-one to pull the strings'. (KC 142)

To be effective ACPC's need resourcing, strategic planning, and commitment. The future role of ACPCs will surely depend on demonstration of effectiveness, in turn related to clarity of role vis-a-vis individual agencies responsibilities. One way of increasing effectiveness will be to improve contact between ACPCs, working in isolation and unco-ordinated. The need for such contact for operational reasons is touched upon in the Aston inquiry. Such contact for policy development and role development is essential.

There is a need too for ACPCs to feel a closer relationship to central Government from whom they clearly look for leadership. A working relationship between central Government and these committees is necessary to enable review and development of function. It is not clear that presently established links are sufficient to do this.

The Liam Johnson inquiry offers a view of the future. It considers that the ACPC should address the essential nature of inter-agency co-operation; joint training; the extent to which the administrative support for the child protection register and the management of case conferences fall short of the recommended guidance; and monitor practice in individual cases. 'If the ACPC is not going to have either an effective budget or any real input into the sort of areas which we think are properly within the ambit of an effective child protection committee, then it seems to us that the ACPC needs to become a much smaller group, which is concerned with reviewing and updating the procedures and remains as a channel through which inter-agency communication, over issues of joint training can take place. If, as we believe, the pattern that we have found here is not dissimilar from that in other parts of the country, then we think the Government too should reconsider the role which it gives to the ACPC in its guidance.' (LJ 9.5–9.9)

the management of individual cases

SECTION 4 THE MANAGEMENT OF INDIVIDUAL CASES

4.1 INTRODUCTION

This section comments on a number of aspects of professional practice: responding to child abuse; recognising child abuse; intervening in cases; issues in relation to fostering placements; and communication and recording.

Analysis of the inquiries demonstrates the difficulty of separating investigation, assessment, and treatment as phases of the professional response. This report seeks to place these within an overall planned response to the child and parents. The inquiries, by concentrating on the work of case conferences make it difficult to address processes of decision making within agencies.

Individual performance

Agency guidelines and policy may 'learn lessons' from previous inquiries into child death, while everyday practice does not. (DA 8.1) The previous review of inquiries said that 'the general picture of practice emerging from the reports is not of gross errors or failures by individuals on single occasions but of a confluence or succession of errors, minor inefficiencies and misjudgments by a number of agencies, together with the adverse effects of substantial factors beyond the control of those involved'. This report confirms that view.

Some reports refer to good practice and some find no serious errors of judgement in the way the professionals handle the case. There is no evidence in some cases that 'something went very wrong' (LJ 2.4 for example). Whilst often acknowledging the criticisms of individuals must not permitted to obscure the wider failings of agencies (CLV 245 for example), the inquiries are more able to find specific failings in the work of individuals, than in the work of agencies, analysis of which tends to be more diffused.

Standards

Inquiries consider reasonable ways of judging the performance of individuals – and generally individuals are judged by what would could have reasonably have been expected of them at the time. Inquiries note the responsibilities of individuals to act to improve the overall service provided to children (DA 8.8) and to individually be prepared to act. The Carlile inquiry makes explicit: 'Whatever the problems and failings of management structure, bad practice is bad practice'. (KC 218)

There is a need for finely tuned decision making. The Kimberley Carlile inquiry judges the quality of social work performed by social workers responding to an anonymous call. 'It is never enough simply to comply with the letter of the state of procedures . . . There is always an overriding professional duty to exercise skill, judgement and care.' (KC 96)

The Aston inquiry notes expectations of professionals and managers are changing and seeks (within the health visiting context) improved and clear standards. (DA 4.46) There is no clear national standard to apply to child protection practice, and such a standard, it strikes the reader of child abuse inquiries, is much needed.

Limits of inquiries

Inquiry reports tend to understate the impact of clients on professionals. Recognition is needed not only of conflicts and problems within professional interaction but also between professionals, parents and children.

Inquiries describe what happened rather than why. They tend not to address the nature of abuse and the reason for it. (CLV 245 and LGP 6.22) Neither do they consider the effectiveness and the appropriateness of strategies used once a problem has been identified, except in the most negative sense.

Limited insight into the circumstances leading to children's deaths is provided by the families after the event. Further research is needed to provide an understanding of what really goes on in families when a child is killed or seriously injured.

A number of inquiries consider the socio-economic environment within which families live and its impact on professionals attempting to help the family. (DA 4.8) They do not seek to consider the effect of socio-economic circumstances on families, let alone as a form of abuse itself.

Doubtless inquiries of the 90s will consider gender, race, and perhaps disability and their relationship to child abuse, adequately. Inquiries of the 80s tend not to address these issues. There are scattered references to physical risk to women social workers or health visitors in the face of aggressive men but little analysis of the roles of men and women in families.

In the Tyra Henry inquiry alone there is a clear view expressed about the impact of racial stereotyping. 'We do not suppose for a second that anybody concerned with social services in Lambeth would have taken a conscious decision that a lower standard of service support was appropriate for poor black clients than for others, but we do think that it may have been an unarticulated and unconscious sense that a woman like Beatrice Henry would find a way of coping, no matter what, that underlay the neglect of Area 5 social services to make adequate provision for her taking responsibility for Tyra.' (TH 7.8)

The Liam Johnson inquiry notes the benefits that would have been derived from a panel member being black, given Liam's father was black, with their shared experience of institutionalised racism. The Beckford inquiry considers that there was a discreet racial dimensions to the case of Jasmine Beckford, although in the end it played little or no part in considerations of the issue of determination. (JB 7) It comments on matters relating to trans-racial fostering (referred to below).

4.2 RESPONDING TO CHILD ABUSE

Blocks to recognition

The inquiries describe at length difficulties professionals have in responding to child abuse. For one reason or another information is not available at an appropriate time, in a useable form and it is not let into the information 'established' about the child and parents. It can be helpful to try to differentiate between types of information require different types of response.

The unknown

There is a need for specialised knowledge. Lack of professional experience expertise and training in child abuse may lead to the failure to identify injury or risk. Inquiries identify knowledge of 'signs of symptoms' of abuse, and knowledge of the law, as key areas.

The known but not fully appreciated

There can be difficulties in classifying information or distinguishing it from a flood of relevant data, for example distinguishing non accidental and accidental injury in a sequence of observed bruising.

Interpretation

Information might not be correctly interpreted. For example, Christine Aston's response to an earlier child's death – that she smothered him – was identified by the social worker as a grief reaction, and this interpretation never challenged (DA).

Objective and subjective information

Failure to distinguish fact and opinion can lead to relevant information not being appreciated. (KMcG 64) Information can be appreciated and misconstrued when the focus is too uncritically on one family member. Health visitors considered Linda Gates to be incapable of actually harming her children – 'this prevented an accurate assessment of the physical injuries suffered by the children over a period of years, and caused the child abuse procedures not to be invoked. The health visitor was too trusting of Miss Gates and should have been more suspicious of the explanations of the injuries and incidents'. (LGP 5.51) The Tyra Henry case illustrates this clearly. The inquiry notes major factors pointing in the opposite direction to that taken by case conference – to look for housing for Claudette on her own – resulting from the social worker's focus on mother, Claudette, and her needs rather than those of Tyra'. (TH)

Unappreciated data

Information may not be appreciated if there is a distrust of the information source – for example relevant information from a police officer at a conference. (TH 10.11) Similarly information may not be appreciated if its source is not valued, for example health visitors information about Jasmine's low weight and apparent under-stimulation being disregarded by doctors and social workers. (JB 8.2)

Information may be disregarded if it was received from a trusted person but of whom positive views are held and it is a surprise, for example information from foster parents about difficulties being experienced. (EJH 2.4.34)

The decoy of dual pathology

Information can also be known and not appreciated if the receiver is decoyed by a different problem. The inquiries are full of instances where, having identified one problem, professionals fail to appreciate another. For example Jasmine Beckford's problem was risk of physical abuse, questions are not asked about her development. (JB 6.9) The only concern about Richard Fraser was him being neglected by his stepmother. Father was violent with stepmother. A possibility of father being violent to Richard was not properly considered. (RF 10) The McGoldrick case was viewed as one of poor parenting. The inquiry says 'that there was an abundance of evidence of poor parenting we have no doubt. This was a case of 'dual pathology' and in concentrating on the poor parenting theme the agencies overlooked or played down a second theme of child abuse'. (KMcG 41)

The superimposition of one view in pathology over another can take place through time. The care order on Tyra Henry followed physical abuse yet the problem became, as it were, the quality of Claudette's parenting. Decisions about the use of the law can set in motion fixed perceptions of the case. And even if dual pathology is identified there may be fixed views about a sole perpetrator and sole victim whereas more than one child may be abused by more than one person (for example CLV 7).

Certainty

Information may not be appreciated by a false sense of security – a certainty about a point of view. One might suggest this of the views of the doctors in Cleveland: 'He considered that his clinical findings were not open to question and that further investigation by other agencies should seek together information to support the diagnosis and consider the future management of the child'. (CLV 8.9.26)

Competing tasks

Pressure from competing tasks can lead to information not being appreciated, for example the approval and support of foster parents can militate against effective listening about the possibility of child protection in the foster household.

The known and not assembled

There are many instances of this noted throughout the inquiries. Information might not be assembled because of perceptions of role and agency function, and is more likely to be ineffectively distributed when several organisations are involved. Information however might not be effectively assembled when procedures set to establish this are not followed through, for example, the police check of the Koseda household. (HK 4.10) Categoric disagreements not adequately resolved between individuals can also lead to a failure to assemble information. Information can be deliberately withheld. (TH). What is needed often is for 'one person to appreciate gaps in information for the veil to be lifted'. (KMCG)

Not fitting the current mode of understanding

Into this category might fall new understanding that children who describe abusive experiences were not fantasising and that children when they talk can, and should, be taken seriously. (CLV 5)

At the heart of this block on information is the workers perception and understanding of children and of the role of social work in child protection. What ought social work to be, influences how it is practised. Professionals attitudes to parents, children and families are affected by their belief system which will influence how they understand what they know, and exclude what does not fit (for example KMcG 26). The principles of clients' self determination, working through parents, keeping families together, on the one hand, and pessimistic perception of alternatives to care within the family on the other, influence understanding and action. (JB 294, LGC 24.7, LJ 3.67)

The Beckford inquiry discusses the 'rule of optimism'. At the inquiry an expert witness, Professor Greenland, stated that 'because the problems are so complex in order to develop enough enthusiasm and enough energy, social workers tend to have a very optimistic view of what can be established. They tend to exaggerate the progress that has been made, and they may see progress where there is no progress. For this reason because of the loss of objectivity, professional supervision is vital . . . the loss of objectivity is a common factor in a management of high risk cases'. However, as pointed out elsewhere, the rule of optimism is the product of a fundamental conflict of values about the relationship between families and the state which receives, at best, a nodding acknowledgement in the Beckford report. It is not that social workers do not know about their authority but rather its exercise is inconsistent with the nature of their role in society (R Dingwall's analysis of the Jasmine Beckford case, which refers to B A Turner's study of Man-Made Disasters (1978). In Modern Law Review Vol 49. July 1986).

Long standing blocks

These blocks on recognition tend to be long standing and cumulative. They can set in motion patterns of relationships whether between professionals or between professionals and families which perpetuate the blocked information flow. For example, the McGoldrick inquiry report identifies three assumptions which appear to have been made at the early stage which influenced the handling of the case. These were: that the problem was poor parenting rather than child abuse; that mothers co-habitee was 'a good character' and a better parent than his mother; and that the family would co-operate in response to intensive surveillance. In fact this was a example of 'dual pathology', the co-habitee 'was able to hoodwink some of those involved as to his true character' and the family did not respond to surveillance, and such surveillance that there was, was 'superficial' or based on incomplete information. (KMcG 41-43)

Involvement of children and parents

One way through these blocks of information is to engage parents and children openly in the investigation assessment and treatment process. The Cleveland inquiry described complaints by parents about professionals. It describes that 'most deeply felt by the parents was the sense of isolation' and the lack of consideration by doctors and social workers. (CLV 2.5.2) The inquiries describe a range of professional relationships with parents, normally one to one and in private. There is little evidence in these cases of parental, let alone child, involvement in planning processes for the child. Throughout the inquiries of the 80s there is little sense of parents and children being involved in planning services for themselves.

A framework of policy and principle: Children's needs and rights

In order to make sense of so much that goes wrong in protecting children it is necessary it to establish a set of principles which clearly places the focus of intervention on the child, and brings the critical and private relationships between child and parent; between child, parent and professional; between field worker and manager; and between agencies, into the open.

The inquiries, as one, state that the primary focus of intervention is the child whose needs and rights are paramount. The Cleveland inquiry is now much quoted: – 'There is a danger that in looking to the welfare of the children believed to be victims of sexual abuse the children themselves may be overlooked. The child is a person and not an object of concern' (CLV 245). The McGoldrick report refers to this statement and says that 'if the phrase 'physical abuse' is substituted for 'sexual abuse', we feel that the amended statement exemplifies one of the main problems of the Karl McGoldrick case'. (KMcG 70) The conduct of professional practice in relation to physically abused children throughout the inquiries supports this view. The following are the Cleveland principles which can apply to all allegedly abused children and their parents.

'We recommend that:

a. Professionals recognise the need for adults to explain to children what is going on. Children are entitled to a proper explanation appropriate to their age, to be told why they are being taken away from home and given some idea of what is going to happen to them.

b. Professionals should not make promises which cannot be kept to a child, and in the light of possible court proceedings should not promise a child that what is said in confidence can be kept in confidence.

c. Professionals should always listen carefully to what the child has to say and take seriously what is said.

d. Throughout the proceedings the views and the wishes of the child, particularly as to what should happen to him/her, should be taken into consideration by the professionals involved with their problems.

e. The views and the wishes of the child should be placed before whichever court deals with the case. We do not however, suggest that those wishes should predominate.

f. Children should not be subjected to repeated medical examinations solely for evidential purposes. Where appropriate, according to age and understanding, the consent of the child should be obtained before any medical examination or photography.

g. Children should not be subjected to repeated interviews nor to the probing and confrontational type of 'disclosure' interview for the same purpose, for it in itself can be damaging and harmful to them. The consent of the child should where possible be obtained before the interviews are recorded on video.

h. The child should be medically examined and interviewed in a suitable and sensitive environment, where there are suitable trained staff available.

i. When a child is moved for home or between hospital and foster home it is important that those responsible for the day to day care of the child not only understand the child's legal status but also have sufficient information to look after the child properly.

j. Those involved in investigation of child sexual abuse should make a conscious effort to ensure that they act throughout in the best interests of the child.

We recommend:

a. The parents should be given the same courtesy as the family of any other referred child. This applies to all aspects of the investigation into the suspicion of child sexual abuse, and should be recognised by all professionals concerned with the family.

b. Parents should be informed and where appropriate consulted at each stage of the investigation by the professional dealing with the child, whether medical, police or social worker. Parents are entitled to know what is going on, and to be helped to understand the steps that are being taken.

c. The position of parents in case conferences (should be one of increased information and involvement).

d. Social Services should confirm all important decisions to parents in writing. Parents may not understand the implication of decisions made and they should have the opportunity to give the written decision to their lawyers.

e. Parents should always be advised of their rights of appeal or complaint in relation to any decision made about them or their children.

f. Social Services should always seek to provide support to the family during the investigation. Parents should not be left isolated and bewildered at this difficult time.

g. The service of the place of safety order on parents should include a written explanation of the meaning of the order, the position of the parents, their continuing responsibilities and rights and advice to seek legal advice'.

Prediction of abuse

It is a point of conjecture within the inquiries, the extent to which child abuse can be predicted. The Beckford inquiry referring to the training of social workers says 'All these skills need to be sustained by an awareness, through knowledge of child development, of parental psychopathology and stress; of child abuse research findings to appraise those cases where the risk factors of abuse outweigh those of separating children from their parents. In short, the ability to detect the 'high risk' cases'. (JB 205) But this is, more realistically, qualified later: 'we do not define 'high risk', mainly because we think that it is not a susceptible definition', and concern is then expressed about the identification of 'false positive' information. (JB 288–289)

It is not possible confidently to predict who will be an abuser, for the potential for abuse is widespread and often triggered by the particular conjunction of circumstances which is unpredictable. Almost anyone with whom the professionals work could be an abuser, and when an incident 'breaks' it is also easy to look back with the confidence of hindsight and to see cues that were missed, small mistakes and tell tale signs. ('A' 2) The Liam Johnson inquiry also takes that view. 'It was said to us before we started hearing evidence that if we could suggest ways in which families like this, who in no way stand out from hundreds of others with whom the agencies deal, could somehow be identified before the tragedy occurs it would be an enormous help. It will be clear from the pages that follow that although we suggest ways in which practice might be improved, we have been unable to suggest any infallible method of spotting potential child killers.' (LF 4.24)

Early warning themes

There are a number of themes running through the inquiries which together, and properly probed, might provide useful warning.

History of unstable, damaging or violent adult relationships

The Koseda inquiry notes that Rosemary Koseda's cohabitation with Nicholas Price 'led to dramatic changes in mother's behaviour'. The inquiry notes 'her relationship with him seems to have been the start of a marked deterioration in her mental state and way of life, which culminated in a serious mental illness after the discovery of Heidi's body early in 1985'. (HK 1.1) Liam Johnson's father had a history of violent relationships with women characterised by violent shifts of mood, and actual violence (LJ 3.5). There might be particular concern when one or more parents are young (TH.LG.SW for example)

Violence outside the family

Violence outside the family is not so strongly reported in the inquiries as violence within, but also should be noted, especially if it is recent or persistent. David Carlile for example shortly before cohabiting with Kimberley's mother had received a three month prison sentence for assault. (KC 49)

A history of violence to children

This theme takes three forms. Firstly the corporal punishment of children in a 'disciplinary' context. Daniel Frankland had been slapped by his pre-adoptive mother at the age of seven months. (CP 3.4.2) Liam Johnson's father gave him 'occasional disciplinary slaps'. (LJ 3.2.1) Richard Fraser's stepmother told the social worker that she had been hit by his father and she has hit the baby on his bottom. (RF 26) 'Smacking (rather than punching) by Linda Gates of her children' is reported. (LGC 37.6) 'She smacked the children, particularly William rather hard.' (LGC 2.16) And most sadly Jason Plischkowsky whose foster mother had admitted smacking him and her own child in disciplinary context, and who died following a fall down stairs, having been smacked by his foster mother (JB 27)

Secondly, the previous abuse of children no longer in the family home. Tyrone Henry suffered 'terrible and permanent injuries. He had fractures of both thighs, retinal haemorrhages, a fracture of the skull and brain damage causing fits . . . resulting in him being blind for life and mentally handicapped'. (TH 2.15) Jason Plischkowsky's eldest sister died of a ruptured liver aged ten months. The father was charged with manslaughter and acquitted but found guilty of neglect. (JP 3) Christine Aston's child Karl died aged ten weeks. The injuries were never satisfactorily explained and his death recorded as a cot death (DA 2.1).

Thirdly previous abuse to children in the household, and the subject child, Jason Caesar, Karl McGoldrick, Jasmine Beckford and others. The Aston inquiry notes Scott's maxim that 'the best indication of dangerousness is past evidence should never be forgotten'. (DA 8.3)

Signs in children

Signs in children are difficult to judge. As the previous study of inquiry reports noted 'a child's demeanour may or may not provide a clue'. The Liam Johnson inquiry notes that 'by the time S (Liam's brother) moved to his father, he had had at least forty one changes of care of household or moves which we have been able to document. L had twenty nine . . . the most remarkable feature in our view, was the ease with which both boys seemed to have settled with their father and A. . . . The only real regression noted in the children was in their speech'. (LJ 3.105) The Beckford inquiry reminds us that the effect of injuries on children will differ. It heard evidence from a consultant orthopaedic surgeon that 'we all react differently to the same injury. Some children will get out of bed and walk normally within a week. Other children with the same fracture will still be limping after a year. There is no way or knowing and there is nothing you or I or the parents can do about it'. (JB 69) The Beckford and Carlile inquiries refer to language development as an important factor in judging the welfare of the child. These inquiries refer also to the importance of judging weight, and development in its wider sense. (JB 74)

Behaviour change

Perhaps more importantly than observations of behaviour at any one time is the detection of changes in children's behaviour over time, perhaps as their carer changes, or as their domestic circumstances change. For example when Linda Gates took the children on a visit to see a previous foster mother . . . 'the appearance of a little girl whose hair was greasy and matted and who appeared thin, pale and withdrawn, shocked Mrs C. Four months previously she had been plump and healthy. Mrs C told us that she took Mary into her bedroom and noted that she had several bruises on the inside of her arms'. (LGC 7.6) The deterioration in Liam Johnson and his brother's behaviour is poignantly documented. In February he had an 18 month developmental check and was getting more sociable and had achieved all his milestones. Two weeks later he was seen by the GP complaining of a sore tongue. By April the boys were said to be rocking and clinging and had bumps and scratches. In May the boys were very distressed, didn't sleep and spent all night rocking and sucking their thumbs. Later in May the mother's sister reported that mother was ill-treating L and was concerned about the deterioration in S's emotional condition. Very frequently he put himself to bed saying that he was poorly. His speech was deteriorating. (LJ 3.47–3.50)

Often it is a question of an observant professional being sensitive to clues and checking them. For example S burst into tears at school in January 1987 because his shoe laces were undone. The teacher noted that he seemed frightened and said his father got angry if they were undone. (LJ 3.116) Richard Fraser did not stand out as presenting special problems. His attendance was very irregular but when he was in class he did not appear to be out of the ordinary. The only distinguishing characteristic was that he ate ferociously. He was very quiet, rarely playing with other children, and did not often speak. (RF 22) In this case more than a clue was provided, the stepmother made him repeat to his teacher every morning when she took him to school 'I was a little bastard all night last night'. (RF 23)

It is difficult to judge, often, whether the behaviour of children is a reflection of abuse, or whether it triggers abuse. Although Daniel Frankland was thriving, Mrs Frankland was 'in despair' because of screaming, demanding and changeable needs. (CP 3.4.2) 'Linda did not take to Lucy. She was a small fragile looking baby.' (LGC 10.2) 'At nursery Christine was upset and said that Doreen had been wetting on purpose and that she was sick in order to be naughty.' (DA 2.131)

Simple observation is no substitute for a thorough assessment. And the wrong conclusions can be drawn about a subject child from the behaviour of siblings 'at the beginning of an interview with the family the team leader noted that Kimberley was withdrawn, sallow, pasty and still. As the interview wore on Kimberley brightened up. The evident cheerfulness and brightness of the other children with whom Kimberley began to play with evident pleasure, distracted the team leader from concluding that this was a case of child abuse'. (KC 110)

Warnings of abuse

Warnings of abuse should be taken seriously from whatever their source. The inquiries describe responses to referrals from a number of sources.

Warnings of abuse from neighbours and friends

The inquiries note problems experienced by neighbours and friends getting their messages heard. Lucy Gates' neighbours, were viewed as malicious and not responded to (LGC 30.1) yet their information was extensive: 'Linda's flat was filthy; her children were dirty and neither properly clothed nor fed; she had an assortment of male visitors; sometimes she left the children alone until the early hours of the morning while she visited a public house; she hit the children excessively and without cause'. The neighbours, it was said, had expressed disapproval of Linda by putting dead mice through her letter box. Their complaints were not taken seriously by the social worker. (LGC 5.17)

A different form of dismissal occurred in the Heidi Koseda case when a vigilant neighbour identified that Heidi was always very hungry and had bruises on her arms and legs. Neighbours had noted the Price/Koseda flat always with the curtains drawn, and in the summer saw Heidi once with her mother 'squinting as if the light was hurting her eyes'. Reports were made to the NSPCC, and not investigated. (HK)

Warnings of abuse from the extended families

The Lambeth social worker in the Doreen Aston case said that Christine's mother and sister had voiced concerns about Christine's baby, she was rough in handling her and did not clean or feed her properly. However the social worker questioned their motives for stating this because there was rivalry between the sisters. She did not observe the child to look neglected or ill and in spite of the concern expressed from the family, the Lambeth social worker did not take them so seriously as to contact the Southwark social worker immediately. (DA 2.123) Similar problems were evident in the McGoldrick case when the paternal grandfather contacted Social Services many times about his grandchildren. 'Mr McGoldrick felt that he was being talked to in a childish manner and repeatedly told that Karl was accident-prone . . . (the principal Social Worker) gave him the impression he was trying to pacify him and was not going to take any positive action'. (KMcG 32) Similarly a neighbour complained and obtained no effective action.

Warnings of abuse from parents

A parent can tell and not be heard. Mr Hall telephoned Social Services admitting that the family were experiencing problems and that the main problem centred on Kimberley. The behaviourial problems exhibited by Kimberley were said by him, to reflect an unacceptance of Mr Hall as her stepfather. In the course of the conversation he admitted to having 'shaken' and 'smacked' Kimberley although he sought to minimise any injuries by attributing them to Kimberley having fallen down while playing. The inquiry notes that 'in short, the call indicated that Kimberley was seriously at risk. It could also have been interpreted as a cry for help from someone who had hitherto been stately declaring that he and his family wanted only to be left alone by Social Services' it did not result in help. (KC 107) Christine Aston's request for reception into care of Doreen, could have been heard as a warning too. (DA)

Statements from children

Finally, children tell. The importance of direct communication with children has been long recognised, as has the difficulty of talking to children who have conflicting and fluctuating feelings. It has also been recognised that the children may try to communicate through actions rather than words and that they cannot be relied on to challenge explanations offered by parents or parent figures, especially when the latter are present. However the theme running through the inquiries of the late 80s is that children do tell, and when they do they must be taken seriously. 'Of the various causes for concern, one related to the response of the Social Services Department to the information that in 1985 a sexual incident had occurred between the foster father and a teenage girl. In spite of the fact that when she was interviewed by her social worker the girl made (and subsequently confirmed repeatedly) serious allegations of sexual assault by the foster father, these allegations were not acted on (mainly because they were not communicated within the agency), nor were the police involved, apparently because there was a belief among a small number of Social Services staff that the girl in question was lying.' ('A' 1)

Children telling begs the question of how to understand, to interpret, what they say.

Clusters of signs

Clusters of signs can be more important than any one on their own – for example in the Beckford case the combination of non attendance at nursery, disharmony between the parents, the fact that Jasmine had not been seen for some time, and the absence of information about Jasmine's health and development. (JB 118) The Heidi Koseda case clusters together the unusual occurrence of a concealed pregnancy; the marked deterioration of the state of the flat; inadequate clothing available for James; earlier involvement with the NSPCC; the absence of Heidi from the family home with little information as to the arrangements made for her; the lack of heating; the inadequate accommodation. 'None of these factors alone or together indicate child abuse per se however they do indicate a family which is subject to a high degree of stress.' (HK 31.15)

The Liam Johnson inquiry notes that the identification of child abuse is often a matter of asking the right questions (LJ 8.16) in order to make sense of what is seen whether 'a classic indicator or a cluster of concerns'.

Critical patterns

In addition to these 'warning signs', there are a number of themes which run through the inquiries and which effect the way in which the cases were, or were not, effectively dealt with. They are described here for three reasons. Firstly, there is a sense in some inquiries that families are passive. That families contain a number of attributes which can be 'known', and they are quietly waiting for 'help'. This is not so. Secondly, to emphasise the need for all those in child protection agencies to consider not only the content but also the process of their relationships to parents and children. Thirdly, recognition needs to be given to professionals problems of dealing with families from day to day. It is for the workers, stressful, sometimes frightening, and sometimes confusing. This is especially so in long-term cases in which roles and perceptions become stuck and fears and fantasies ebb and flow. These patterns illustrate how difficult, demanding and stressful working with families can be especially when role is unclear. Most of the inquiries are into child abuse deaths in long-term cases.

Recurrent incidents and concerns

Recurrence of injuries and the importance of identification of recurrent abuse, are well established themes. Important too is the need to establish patterns within biographies by careful sharing of information and record checking. In April 1987 the Southwark social worker spoke to Christine Mason's mother and referred to Christine's request on 16th April for Doreen to be taken into care. Mrs Mason said that Christine had made a similar request that day. Had the Southwark social worker had the Berkshire social work records she would have noted that Christine had made a request for Karl to enter care at about the time when the injuries noted post mortem could have been inflicted (to him). (DA 2.159)

Resistance to professional intervention

Resistance can take a variety of forms. It needs to be dealt with in order to avoid collusion or drift. The Beckford inquiry notes Morris Beckford's resentment at the intrusion social workers in his private life. (JB 116) The Charlene Salt inquiry describes a case discussion when the need for regular stripping and weighing of Charlene was to be discussed with the parents. They did not arrive as they were out in their new car. The inquiry notes that despite the further 'glaring example of non co-operation' the matter was not referred back to court, as the court had requested. (CS 12) Liam Johnson's mother did not appreciate the befriending approach of her social worker. The inquiry notes that 'it is unrealistic to think that every social worker can or ought to establish that sort of rapport with every user of their services. There will always be those who, like the mother, clearly see social workers as a resource to provide money and other practical necessities'. (LJ 3.60) 'The father had been frank about not wanting social work help. His own family had never been involved with Social Services and he regarded involvement with them as something to be ashamed of . . . At no time was he hostile, truculent or obstructive. No one was refused admission to the house and the children never missed appointments.' (LJ 3.111) The inquiry also notes 'it is very difficult for services to work effectively with those who have a high level of social skills, reasonable confidence in parenting, keep appointments and take their children to the clinic regularly or when asked. Such families are extremely unlikely to confide in any agency professional'. (LJ 420)

Coping with these problems needs a structured and planned approach. It is important not to be beguiled by 'false positive' information: Richard's father and stepmother were willing to co-operate with the school and encouraged teachers to call in at their homes if there were any problems. This was taken as a sign of improvement. It was then decided not to inspect Richard at the school medical in July as it was considered that this might upset improved relations with the family, the medical would take place during the next school term. (RF 30)

Lying and deceitfulness

A recurring theme, is the extent to which parents will lie and seek to deceive professional workers. On one level it might be understandable on another it can have more sinister consequences. The Carlile inquiry describes the family turning up unexpectedly in response to a threatening letter from the team leader and a phone call by Mr Hall the previous day, admitting problems. 'The team leader had been impressed, he told us, by the initiative parents had taken in coming to him, instead of waiting for the home visit by him. The irony of that observation, then and now, is that in fact the Carlile's were coming to him, and not him to them, in order to conceal, rather than to reveal.' (KC 111) Those working in the field of child abuse must always be on their guard against the risk of seeing what they want to believe. Social workers must attempt to verify verifiable facts presented during child abuse investigations.

About the last visit to Jasmine Beckford the inquiry concludes that 'the visit was stage managed by the Beckford parents who had been given five days notice of the impending visit and thus had an opportunity to arrange the siting of the children and the unrevealing clothing worn by Jasmine. Indeed Morris Beckford said as much in his written statement to the inquiry'. (JB 126) Social workers 'must always be sceptical of the manipulative acts of abusing parents'. (KC 99)

Lying and plausibility are noted too in other inquiries. (LJ 3.28 & TH 23) The social worker in the Tyra Henry case recorded that she was 'very annoyed at Claudette for concealing so much information but glad to have the information. – This will not affect our plans' the fact of concealment was not explored. (TH 3.33) There is a distinct change of tone, the Tyra Henry inquiry notes, in relation to Claudette Henry's non co-operation when the second social worker takes over. The firmer approach, the inquiry believed, resulted in Claudette beginning to show signs of taking Social Services involvement seriously. (TH 3.38) Examples of lying are also to be found in the Lucy Gates and Charlene Salt inquiry reports. (CS 10. LGC 55.2)

Spotting deception is difficult but imperative. In the Carlile case, Kimberley had not been seen for a month despite some efforts by the team leader, the social worker. Her place at a nursery had not been taken up. The inquiry considered that 'how the team leader failed to see the blindingly obvious (severe physical and emotional abuse) is explicable only by the fact that he was blinded by his incompetence in assessing clear deception by abusing parents, something all social workers must be constantly alive to'. (KC 47)

Failure to attend day nursery or school

Beverly Lorrington removed Jasmine Beckford from day nursery. For two months Jasmine was out of sight. The panel regarded that as highly significant because the first repetition of child abuse to Jasmine took place around the time of the November 1982 case conference. (JB 117) The inquiry notes that from 8th September 1983, the day before Jasmine's last school attendance begins the evasive action by the Beckford's, and the panel concludes that the child abuse restarted about that time. (JB 123 also KC, RF, LJ)

Non access

In the case of Claire Haddon regular visits over a three week period by the premature baby midwife, health visitor and social worker were followed by consecutive aborted visits. The inquiry recommended that guidance should be established to assist when visits to children at risk do not result in access. (CH 6.4) The Salt inquiry notes that the first health visitor had great difficulty in gaining access to the house and regarded it as not surprising, as 'she was probably seen by the Salts as a much more dangerous person than the social worker since the health visitor was wanting frequently to weigh and examine the baby'. (CS 12)

The inquiry describes attempts by the family to shut out the outside world keeping the curtains constantly drawn and trying to have no contact with neighbours. (CS 5) A similar description appears in the Koseda case 'the family seemed metaphorically to have raised the drawbridge around their flat'. (HK 1.9) This resulted in a health visitor recording a 'not known' and in consequence no further attempt was made to contact the family. There was no contact with the GP either, and as Heidi was not yet attending any nursery there were no statutory services in touch with the family who might have noticed signs of what was happening to her at this crucial point. (HK 1.9) This was followed by Rosemary Koseda giving birth to a daughter at home having received no ante natal care and that the pregnancy not being known to the health service. (HK 1.19)

Failing to gain access can result in a reduction of professional services for one reason or another. The Aston inquiry describes social workers failing to gain access to Doreen although discussions could take place at the front doorstep with Roy Aston. (DA 2.5. 2-5.3) Later there followed a sequence of no access visits by health visitor and social worker. Each looked to reduce contact with the family. Case conference minutes recorded the Social Services team leader as pointing out 'help has always been regarded as intervention and surveillance by Christine and Roy, so a reduction in help is probably wise in that it could be seen as stating there were positives for the family'. (DA 2.117)

Whereabouts unknown

In two cases women disappeared during pregnancy and one after giving birth. (DA 2.16, CH 2.7 and CH 2.15) A feature of the Aston case is Christine's uncertain whereabouts and movement between boroughs. A section of the report is headed 'Where were Christine and Doreen living'? It suggests that serious problems of liaison could have been reduced had the opportunity been taken for 'early allocation and the systematic and planned approach to the management of the case adopted immediately the case came to notice of the area'. (DA 2.40)

The Liam Johnson inquiry describes as a complicating factor in the management of the case 'that on each occasion when the children were known to be victims of some assault, . . . they moved to a different part of the country and to completely different domestic situation. Thus Sheffield and other Yorkshire agencies were dealing with the situation of a mother who had separated herself and her children from an allegedly violent partner . . . Similarly, when it was the mother who was expressing concern about her own potential for violence towards the children she took them to the father and left them there . . . the effect of the move was once more to remove the children from the person from whom they were at most immediate risk . . . On each occasion it is impossible to say that the decision to see how the new situation developed was the wrong one. On the contrary on each occasion in the childrens' interest it was probably right'.
(LJ 5.3-5)

Claudette Henry went missing and the inquiry could not establish where she might be, and 'before the next planned conference could take place Tyra was dead. There is very little on record about her in the last three months of her life. We think it probable that her mother was spending substantial periods of time with her in Andrew Neil's company'. (TH 4.26)

Violent behaviour

This may be self directed. Nicholas Price, 'when the consultant wished to induce labour, . . . became disturbed, refused to leave Rosemary and banging his head against the wall. There was no evidence of violence towards anyone other than himself, but the incident is clearly recalled by hospital staff'. (HK 1.4)

Linda Gates threatened to break a bottle and 'to push in' the home help's face. (LGC 4.5) A head teacher was intimidated by Richard Fraser's stepmother and concerned that an external examination of Richard would provoke strong adverse reaction from stepmother. It was agreed to pursue a low profile 'in school' assessment. Richard never returned to Hillmead School after the medical examination and the assessment never took place. (RF 106) The social worker was attempting to give support to Richard's family and visited the house regularly 'but it wasn't easy because of a fear of atmosphere of antagonism towards her. She felt herself to be at risk, and expressed her anxiety to case conference, when it was agreed that she would continue on the case on the basis of 'low profile' visits of a routine nature'. The inquiry notes that the social worker 'clearly wasn't safe with Richard's family, and asked to be taken off the case'. (RF 62)

Social services and school staff found Nigel Hall intimidating. 'The effects of fear of violence are likely very hard to identify . . . If, as is the case, some social workers are to ashamed after being attacked to report the incident and are even then inclined to blame themselves, how much more unlikely must be that they will admit to the feeling of uneasiness before any violence has occurred. It is not easy to admit to being afraid; social workers must, for their sake and for their clients sake. . . . It is only too easy to find other reasons for doing something, or not doing something, when the real reason is that we are afraid to do it. . . . Every effort must be made to make sure that the social workers assessment, on which might hinge the safety of a child, is not disarmed by the possibility of violence or the fear of its possibility. We encourage social workers to be straight, open and frank with their clients when investigating possible cases of child abuse . . . and to speak out if they are fearful for their own safety or if they consider their performance as a social worker is being handicapped by fear of violence.' (KC 197) The Cleveland inquiry notes that anger, aggressive and destructive behaviour and the possibility of violent impulsive reactions should be faced. The social worker needs to maintain an open, structured relationship with the family. (CLV 13.18)

Pressure from within the family not to disclose

The Cleveland inquiry notes how many children who have been subject to sexual abuse were under pressure by the perpetrator not to tell; there may be threats of violence with the child or that the perpetrator will commit suicide or be taken away from home. (CLV 6) The Liam Johnson inquiry described pressure within the adult relationship resulted in a woman not reporting (LJ 4.11) and the Reuben Carthy inquiry described extensive sighting by members of the extended family on Reuben that went unreported. (RC 31) In the case of Reuben Carthy the motive may have been collusion. Family pressure and collusion are not mutually exclusive and it is essential to find out what is happening.

A period of silence

'It is a characteristic of many of the cases in which a child dies at the hands of a parent that it emerges that no one from any of the agencies saw the child during the last weeks of his life. That pattern is repeated here although to a lesser degree than in many cases. After the death this becomes significant. Pre-death the workers may not have even realised it that it was happening.' (LJ 4.23 also DA 2.188, RF 68) The silence is never absolute but through misperceptions, misunderstanding and a failure to identify what is happening within the structured approach to the case, and the power of what families do, effective contact with the child does not happen.

The deaths of the children

The deaths were brought to the attention of the authorities in various ways, one found, others reported direct to hospital, one via a GP. Contact with the authorities was made by third parties, spouses, and one anonymously. No particular pattern is to be found.

Common themes

Other clusters of factors though, do emerge. Four of the children died in foster care in each case convictions of the foster mother followed. Of the remaining thirteen, twelve died following injuries, one of neglect. However malnourishment and neglect were contributory factors in three of the other children. Over half the children had suffered previous injuries. There were typically delays in seeking medical help, and the families who most delayed were generally the families who had been deceiving and avoiding the authorities. The violence was inflicted in some cases by father or father substitute alone, in others by mother alone. There are a clustering of cases, however, six, in which both stepfather and mother were convicted. In all cases where a stepfather was present in the household, he was convicted.

Events prior to the death

Inquiries vary in the extent of the information about events leading to the death. Where events have been able to be pieced together they are a sobering tale. Richard Fraser, for example died following an assault. On the Friday before he died on the Sunday he apparently fell asleep in the playground during the lunch break. It was decided that he should remain at school, and he slept through the afternoon. The inquiry emphasises the impact of a home environment where there was such violence between adults and describes his condition seeming to deteriorate both physically and psychologically during the last months of his life. (RF 3) Jasmine Beckford's is a story of psychological battering, chronic undernourishment, and assaults. Karl McGoldrick died from an assault, there had been previous referrals from neighbours and family that were not thoroughly investigated. (KMcG 56) Reuben Carthy suffered severe and extensive injuries of recent origin, probably occurring in more than one episode, old injuries were also identified. He was killed by his mother. He was seen by his mother, an aunt, a sister-in-law and a male visitor in a state of extreme pain, and no action was taken to alert the medical authorities until the child was apparently dead. (RC 28)

Doreen Aston died well nourished, as a result of bleeding inside the skull following a blow to the back of the head. She had other injuries including a fracture that had occurred not less than a month before her death, but could have been as old as six months. (DA 2.216) The Tyra Henry inquiry pieces together events prior to Tyra's death in considerable detail. There were arguments between Tyra's mother and a cohabitee about Tyra misbehaving, when she did Andrew Neil would hit her hard, usually on the bottom or the backs of the legs. On a Friday in August Tyra angered Neil by wetting on the floor or bed. He picked her up, hit her, swore at her and dropped her on the floor when she screamed. Her mother tried to intervene and Neil turned on her. Further violence occurred over the next few days. On the Wednesday there was a fight between Neil and Claudette in which he hit Tyra. He picked her up and threw her onto the bed with such violence that she struck her head on the headboard. Claudette went out and during that time Neil attacked Tyra, biting, scratching and striking her repeatedly. (TH 5.7-9)

Lucy Gates died following the fall of an electric fire onto her having been left on her own by her mother . (LCG 19) Heidi Koseda died of starvation, the precise date of her death is not known. Death took place some three to eight weeks before the body was found by the police. She was deprived of food and drink in the beginning to punish her for being greedy; she then refused to accept food although it was offered, and finally died. There were no other signs of injury. (HK 1.18)

Deaths in foster care

The deaths in foster care are less well documented by the inquiries. Christopher Pinder suffered multiple injuries and died the following day. His foster/pre-adoptive mother pleaded guilty to manslaughter with diminished responsibility. Shirley Woodcock died of a head injury following a fall to a mat.

Medical evidence

The Liam Johnson case shows the difficulty of making sense of medical evidence. He had suffered injuries, his stomach was empty and the experts agreed that he had been dead for at least six and possibly as much as 12 hours before he was taken to hospital. Medical evidence failed to establish conclusively the cause of the injuries. Lessons from this for less extreme cases is the need to recognise the complexity of conclusive medical diagnosis of physical abuse.

Retrospective judgement

Three separate comments can be made. Firstly information obtained retrospectively from court evidence and other previously silent family members, provides a quality of understanding of what happened not found otherwise in the inquiries. Much greater detail is needed if we are to understand more fully the circumstances in which children die.

Secondly, one notes the tendency of the families, not only immediately prior to the death but for a time before, to both avoid and not seek help. On the other hand we read about occasions where people tell but are not listened to.

Thirdly, to help deal with the problems noted between professional workers and families, increased parent and child involvement in planning what happens to them is much needed. A way to tackle this is afforded by the commitment in government guidelines following the Cleveland inquiry to increase parental and child involvement in planning the services they receive, reinforced by the provisions of the Children Act 1989.

4.3 INVESTIGATION

A problem in analysing the child abuse inquiries is that the boundaries between the stages of intervention are unclear, both in practice and in the inquiries themselves. For example, in practice, the Cleveland inquiry noted that there was confusion whether some interviews were being conducted to ascertain the facts or for therapeutic purposes or a mixture of both, and elsewhere it refers to the boundaries between diagnostic/assessment work and longer term therapeutic work objectives being often confused. (CLV 4.148) Within the inquiries, for example, Kimberley Carlile inquiry repeatedly seems to use 'investigations' and 'assessment' inconsistently and interchangeably.

In real life, these stages are not clear, and rigid formulation can be unhelpful and militate against 'new information' being let in. 'Referrals', or in long term cases 'new information', can arrive at any time. Analysis of the inquiries suggests most strongly that any intervention by any professional requires a clear purpose, defined from the start. In this analysis, the purpose of investigation is taken to be to obtain information to establish whether a child is in need of protection, and to allow preliminary planning to be undertaken in relation to her needs and to allow additional information to be taken into account.

Two uses of the word 'planning' are in current usage. In one usage, after 'referral' when new information provides concern that a child may need protection, 'planning' is deciding who is going to do what in the investigation. In addition, after a full assessment has taken place a 'child protection plan' would describe the provision of services on the basis of the needs of the child and an understanding on available or potential resources in the family.

Two acts are needed on receipt of referral information in order to intervene effectively – firstly the information has to be recognised as about child protection, and secondly strategic decisions are needed between agencies about who is going to do what in response to it.

The primary purpose of an investigation is to protect the child.

Referrals

How the initial referral or complaint is received and understood is critical to the protection process. The Koseda inquiry notes the need of sympathetic assurance and skilled interviewing to identify and help (the caller) to articulate the basis for her concern. Callers must feel they are being taken seriously in what for them might be a state of nervousness and uncertainty. (HK 2.22)

Inquiries address the receipt of anonymous calls. The Carlile inquiry states that where necessary callers anonymity must be protected. Refusal by Social Services Departments to accept referrals unless callers agree to give their names and addresses and allow these to be passed on to members of the family being investigated, whilst being open, straight and frank, is incompatible with the interests of children. (KC 203)

Evaluating information

There is the problem of deciding whether information – allegations or even rumours – are sufficiently serious and well founded to initiate inquiries. A number of reports contain examples of information (often later substantiated) being regarded as malicious (LGC) or misguided. (KMcG) The evaluation of parents' self-referrals can also be difficult. Reuben Carthy's mother referred herself to Social Services. There was later a dispute about what was said but the social worker's view was that mother stated that she 'sometimes felt like hitting the children and might do this if she was forced to give up her employment and stop at home to look after the children full time'. It was well known within the community that scarce resources of nursery places might be available if suggestions were made to the Social Services that the child was a risk. The inquiry is concerned that the degree of investigation which takes place should be so wholly dependent on what might be 'an accidental terminology in expressions by the care-giver'. It recommends that agencies establish a practice providing that in cases in which a parent or care-giver expresses a risk of future abuse or present abuse with no available evidence of actual injury the case is referred to a senior officer for consultation, and that arrangements should be made for the children of the family to be seen. (RC 84-89)

Record keeping

A firm point coming through inquiries is the need to properly record referral information. There are examples of information not being recorded or being recorded incorrectly. (DA 2.131, HK 1.14) This was particularly an issue in the Heidi Koseda case in whch the recorded message showed a number of basic mistakes for example absence of details about the informant; the message recorded the concern of the informer but is devoid of any details about the child or the cause of concern. (HK 2.27)

Response

Inquiries emphasise the need for a response, and that it is timely. It is important that when concerns are express they reach the person who can take action to protect the child. In the Claire Haddon inquiry there is an example of referral by letter which was never received because it was improperly addressed. (CH 3.6.2)

Failed response

There are examples of failure to respond when information is received. The Heidi Koseda inquiry records that 'the sequence of events with which the panel has been mainly concerned began with a telephone call to the NSPCC on 3rd September 1984 made by a neighbour of the Price/Koseda family expressing their concern about possible ill treatment of both Heidi Koseda and her brother. This referral was never investigated; thus neither the area review committee procedures nor the rules of the NSPCC were followed. The Liam Johnson inquiry reflects upon the facts that no one interviewed father at the time of mother's allegations about him assaulting S, Liam's brother. 'There are many situations in which the Social Services Department has to act on unsubstantiated allegations. The difficulty in that is if evidence is not collected at the time of the allegation, it seldom will be'. (LJ 3.24 also KC 97, RC 133)

Responding to child sexual abuse

However there is a need to recognise that 'child sexual abuse has different characteristics from physical abuse. It requires cautious measured intervention which will allow the risks of a false positive finding to be balanced against those of a false negative, and which will produce the evidence required by the court to secure the future welfare of the child concerned'. (CLV 4.189) Witnesses to the inquiry emphasised that the speed and nature of the response will depend on the way in which the child's needs came to light. The distinctions were drawn between those cases which presented in a clear way with circumstantial or physical signs accompanied by specific allegations by a child, and those cases where suspicions were raised by signs or behaviour but there was not a complaint by a child or third party. In the latter cases it was agreed that intervention should be planned in a more measured way. (CLV 13.7) Where an allegation by a child was accompanied by primary medical signs allowing a definitive conclusion to be drawn, the case would need to be referred directly to the police and\or Social Services, however. (CLV 249)

Minimise trauma to the child

The investigation must be sensitive to the child and reduce to a minimum any trauma to him or her. This should effect decisions about intervening at night, and decided on a suitable place to see the child. (CLV 11.41)

'Disclosure' and 'denial'

Problems of 'denial' are turned on their head in the Cleveland inquiry's consideration of disclosure interviews. A fundamental problem of the disclosure approach is that inherent in the concept is that there is something to disclose. The alternative to 'disclosure' is seen as 'denial'. The question of disclosure interviews is considered at length and careful guidance is then offered. The following views were indorsed by the inquiry:

'1. The undesirability of calling them disclosure interviews, which precluded the notion that sexual abuse might not have occurred.

2. All interviews should be undertaken only by those with some training, experience and aptitude for talking with children.

3. The need to approach the interview with an open mind.

4. The style of the interviews should be open ended questions to support and encourage the child in free recall.

5. There should be where possible only one and not two interviews for the purpose of evaluation an interview should not be too long.

6. The interview should go at the pace of the child and not of the adult.

7. The setting for the interview must be suitable and sympathetic.

8. It must be accepted that at the end of the interview the child may have no information to support the suspicion of sexual abuse and the position will remain unclear.

9. There must be careful recording of the interview and what the child says, whether or not there is a video recording.

10. It must be recognised that the use of selective techniques makes great difficulties in subsequent court proceedings.

11. The great importance of adequate training for those engaged in this work.

12. A 'facilitative' interview should be treated as a second stage.' (CLV 12.34)

The benefit of this guideline is that it offers clear demarcation between investigation and assessment, and notwithstanding matters of urgency is a guide for interviews with all children who are suspected to have suffered abuse.

Medical examination

Children who are suspected of suffering child abuse must be medically examined. The need is emphasised for a paediatrician to become involved when children are seen in an accident and emergency department with suspicious injuries. (JB 77, LJ 6.22-24) The Cleveland inquiry sets standards for doctors undertaking examinations in the context of child sexual abuse. These have a more general application. Doctors should recognise the importance: of taking a full medical history and making a thorough medical examination; of making where appropriate investigations; of completing full and accurate medical records which should provide the information for the protective agencies and on occasions the courts. Those records should be made at the time of examination of preparing statements for police purposes and/or for Social Services or NSPCC. The inquiry also discusses the important question of parental consent to medical examination. The approach of the doctor examining any child must show consideration, kindness, and provide an explanation of the steps being taken. But in addition with the older child of appropriate age and understanding his/her consent should also be obtained. (CLV 11.40)

The children must be seen

Inquiries emphasise that the children involved must be seen. The Kimberley Carlile inquiry describes 'Towards the end of a visit the team leader was permitted to peep through the small glass panel at the top of the door to one of the children's bedrooms'. (KC 115) Clearly seeing the child must be in a meaningful social context. The Charlene Salt inquiry considered that when there are reasonable grounds for thinking that a child may be injured, a social worker or other professional should insist on seeing the child undressed. (CS 17) Moreover, not only the subject child but all children in the family should be seen. (KC 96 & KMcG 62) The Koseda inquiry emphasises this most strongly. This emphasis is for two reasons: 'first the conditions which may have lead to the abuse of the named child may very well apply to other children of the family; this is more particularly the case where one child is a stepchild, which effectively Heidi was. Second, telephone messages (about named children) are frequently inexact and such a routine procedure would provide a valuable safe guard'. It notes failure to see all the children even when executing a warrant – the room in which Heidi was lying dead was not entered having been said to be treated with chemicals. (HK 34.8)

Talking to and listening to children

It is also essential that the child or children are spoken to. This is discussed at great length in the Cleveland inquiry which emphasises that the child must be taken seriously. (12.1) There is no information that children were interviewed as part of investigations in other inquiries, the McGoldrick report clearly considers this necessary in physical abuse cases too. (KMcG 70)

Persistence

Investigation clearly requires persistence especially when there are problems gaining access to children. The Carlile inquiry notes drawbacks in sending letters rather than taking personal action. A letter might have precipitated more abuse; and it might not achieve the required results by increasing parental resistance, in this case to taking the child to the doctor. (KC 104-106) It notes the need for persistence too if the family is seen. Two social workers visited the Hall/Carlile household and were told by parents that the children were in bed. The inquiry considered that despite the determined resistance the workers might have said 'in not so many words we are not leaving until we have seen the two younger children', and that a subsequent visit should have been carried out that evening. (KC 98)

There is also a need for persistence in the checking of explanations given, especially in the context of resistance on prior occasions. Again the Carlile inquiry notes that 'those working in the field of child abuse must always be on their guard against the risk of seeing what they want to believe . . . at any meeting with the family it is vital to talk directly to the children themselves (always assuming that the children are capable of understanding); if child abuse is suspected, the parents must be confronted with that suspicion; where the suspicion is denied the parental explanation for suspicion being unfounded must be put to the test'. (KC 112) 'The activity to the Social Services Department showed grave misjudgment . . . it was evident that the investigation was sadly at fault and too superficial.' (KMcG 46-50)

Levels Of Proof

Proof requires evidence. It needs to be made available. The Beckford inquiry describes a circumstance in which medical input into the management of the child abuse case was focused entirely on the orthopaedic condition of both the children and the ophthalmic condition of Louise. 'There was an absence of information relating to child development . . . it was only at the court hearing in September that information from a consultant paediatric radiologist was available – and the full nature of Jasmine's injuries revealed.' (JB 68)

Cumulative evidence

Evidence is cumulative; the level of proof in care proceedings is not the same as in criminal cases. In the McGoldrick case the question of evidence and proof figures largely. It considers an application for a supervision order in the context of successive injuries to Karl. The professionals' view was that his injuries were more likely to be due to poor standards of care than abuse, and that therefore removal of the children from their parents should not be contemplated. Abusive incidents continued. The inquiry identified seventeen critical incidents between September 1985 and December 1986. 'Three further episodes occurred which should have raised strong suspicions of non accidental injury, even taken in isolation. The case conferences, however, seemed to have failed to realise that the cumulative underlined implications of these three episodes; the significance of each was greatly increased by those preceding it . . . We conclude that overwhelming evidence of deliberate child abuse accumulated progressively and the frequent allegations which supported this, were not properly investigated or even ignored.' (KMcG 57-8)

Investigating deaths

Infant deaths in suspicious circumstances should be fully investigated. The Aston inquiry says 'We do not wish to imply that more could have been done in this case but we emphasise that, especially where there is a likelihood of, or in Christine's case, a stated intention of further pregnancy, every effort should be made to investigate the parenting of the deceased child in the light of injuries inflicted prior to the death but discovered post mortem. It cannot be assumed that because criminal proceedings are not taken in respect of the child death, there will not be serious cause for concern as to future parenting capacity which might give rise to legal intervention at the time of birth'. (DA 2.13)

The Aston inquiry emphasises the need for pre-birth case conferences to share information and to consider new information relating to the current family situation, the effect of the death on the parent attitudes to ante natal care, and so on. The problem remains how to identify these cases effectively.

4.4 ASSESSMENT

The need for assessment is considered in government guidelines, and established in professional practice, as an essential of moving from receipt of referral or investigation to treatment. Yet 'assessment' is consistently missing from the practice of the cases described in the inquiries. The inquiry reports remark upon the absence, but whilst offering many recommendations about communication and case conferences say little about the process of assessment itself. The term assessment seems to have two uses, firstly referring to the pooling and sharing of information between professionals, and secondly face to face contact with children and parents. The inquiries tend to refer to assessment in the former sense. The Cleveland inquiry is an exception.

Assessment and planning

The relationship between a thorough assessment and planning is established. For example, Shirley Woodcock was part of a family well-known to the authority. It should have been possible to establish a clear approach to the social work service to be offered to the family. Instead the response appears to have been unfocused and unplanned . . . Opportunities were missed to impose some order on the case and provide a stronger basis for future work . . . If positive and focused assistance based on a proper assessment had been provided from the early stages of the case, evidence might have emerged which would have provided the basis of legal intervention at an earlier stage. (SW 9.2-5)

Complete and accurate information

Information should be as complete as possible and all potentially useful sources of information should be identified and considered together. The study of inquiries in the 80s confirms the view held of those of the 70s that 'The most common picture to emerge from the reports is one of information scattered between a number of agencies, and never systematically collated to form a more complete view than individual workers could achieve separately'.

Active information gathering

Inquiries lay considerable emphasis on the use of continuous and accurate written records (see below). Effort must be taken to research records. The Claire Haddon report notes that 'greater priority should have been given to researching Haddon's earlier history, a knowledge of which might have injected greater caution before the decision was made to support J remaining with him'. (CH 3.3.3) There is value in making chronologically based assessments of information available which would enable sequences of information relating to the progress of the children in foster homes, for example, to be properly collated. (LGP 6.14) The Lucy Gates inquiry goes on to note, however, that more is needed: an accurate record of incidents and developments, systematic supervision of the social worker and periodic case conferences should have enabled an objective judgement to be made on whether Linda Gates was then capable of looking after the two children. (LGC 37.5)

The pooling of information should not be seen as a passive act, it requires actively establishing and maintaining contacts. There is benefit in positive information being shared by social worker and health visitor rather than 'leaving the situation negatively to the effect that they would exchange information if either had reason for heightened concern'. (CH 3.8.3)

The Liam Johnson inquiry expressed concern that the case conference became the focal point of the work rather than the assessment. 'We were struck by the fact that in both London and Sheffield, the social workers made assessments of the family and then collected the background information for the conference . . . Under the prevailing system, the assessment is made that the children are alright and the question is then whether anything in the background information is sufficiently compelling to undermine that assessment of the current situation.' (LJ 6.14) The inquiry recommends that wherever possible, Social Services should obtain information from other agencies before making an assessment of the children's situation rather than afterwards. (LJ R1)

Clear transmission

It is essential that any information transmitted is complete and accurate. The inquiries abound with examples of the transmission of incomplete and inaccurate information. For example, Lucy Gates' health records were found to be confusing because 'they give four different figures for her birth weight . . . further, there were discrepancies in the maternity departments records concerning the base line measurements relating to her length at birth and her head circumference, thereby making subsequent charting of her growth difficult'. (LGC .10) An unpublished inquiry report suggests that a clear framework for assessment is necessary if the focus on the child is to be maintained. Such a framework should help in identification of gaps in information that need filling, and possible sources of missing information.

Corroboration where possible

Inquiries give emphasis to the need to corroborate information. Information from clients, family and neighbours might be particularly unreliable as they may have reasons for painting rosier pictures that the facts may warrant. But so too, do workers' perceptions of the case need checking on a basis of fact rather than opinion.

Focus of the assessment

'The first consideration in an intervention is the welfare of the child. The second should be a full assessment of the family. It is absolutely essential that those involved with the family, social workers, and others conduct the fullest assessment of the family background. A full family history is shown repeatedly to be of vital importance. It is necessary to assess the family by looking at the parents individually, the parents relationship, the vulnerability of the child, the child situation in the family, the family social situation, their contacts with the extended family etcetera as well as considering and recording the family's perspective of events which set the referral in motion.' (CLV 13.13) The Cleveland inquiry emphasises that balanced judgements cannot be made without careful appraisal. It considers that in Cleveland there had been a situation when important judgements were based on the child's and parents' reaction to the present rather than any analysis or understanding of their functioning as individuals or as a family unit. The inquiry regarded as 'a sad fact that in very few of the social work files of the families seen by us, was there evidence of social workers taking a full social history of the family so as to inform their own views and decisions and more widely, those of the case conferences they attended'.
(CLV 4.158-159) The inquiry places emphasis both on historical and the here-and-now information.

Psycho-social and medical assessment

Inquiries note the need to relate a psycho-social to a medical assessment. There is a stated need when relating assessments by different agencies to ensure that the purpose of the assessment is clear, and that adequate briefing information is shared. (DA 2.147)

In addition to assisting the assessment of risk and the needs of the child now, such assessments can provide a baseline against which to assess progress. The Richard Fraser inquiry was unable to ascertain why, when Richard was in hospital or in care during 1975, no agency took the opportunity to undertake a developmental assessment 'this could have ascertained his mental, physical and psychological condition, and would have provided a valuable baseline for future assessments'. (RF 16)

Health visitor assessment

Health visiting practice demands assessment of need and the formation of child care objectives. 'This involves actively seeking out known health and social records to provide a history, and analyzing the information. Following assessment, a health care plan must be recorded within accompanying time scale. On going surveillance enables evaluation of the care given, and necessary modification to be made to the plan. This also serves the purpose of drawing attention to any deflection from preset aims and objectives. No health care plan was ever made for Kimberley.' (KC 166)

Percentile charts

Both the Beckford and Carlile inquiries emphasise the use of percentile charts to inform developmental assessment. They note inconsistency of use. Consistent use, for example, would have indicated a very welcome and dramatic improvement in Kimberley's development in a foster home, but would also have thrown light on her lack of proper development while in the care of her mother. 'The failure to correlate these measurements with previous data indicates an absence of any system or person effectively monitoring Kimberley's disordered progress.' (KC 43)

Structured and focused intervention

The advantage of such a structured and purposeful approach to assessment is that it provides a check against inappropriate focus on one aspect of a family's problem, or any inappropriate member of the family. It also provides a basis for identifying all possible sources of harm. The McGoldrick inquiry notes that concerns about Karl's sister were ignored. 'The allegations made by Karl's sister, and her grandparents concerns about her, based on these allegations and their own observations, seem never to have been fully investigated. There is no evidence of any inquiry into Mark Knowles' treatment of her. She was not included in the supervision order. Bearing in mind the overall ambience in Karl's own history, we conclude that these omissions should never have occurred. The fact that proper investigation might have led to a case conference in respect of his sister could in our view have changed the outcome in Karl's case.' (KMcG 62)

In the Aston case a case conference decided that Doreen should have a developmental check. The inquiry says 'In our opinion this decision, which concentrated on Doreen's development, paid little attention to the problem of the relationship between Christine and Doreen. The case conference proceeded on the basis that either Doreen would 'fail' the check or Christine would fail to take her to the clinic. In either case there would be a basis for further action. Contingency plans based on the outcome that Doreen 'passed' should have been made for the continuing assessment of the relationship between Doreen and her mother, and between Christine and Roy'. (DA 6.41)

Planning for legal intervention can skew perceptions unless 'purpose' prevents all sources of harm to be identified and kept in mind. An unpublished inquiry notes that the decision to place the application for the first interim order on the adults' neglect of the children rather than physical abuse, which was determined by the lack of medical evidence appears to have detrimentally influenced future work in this case. With hindsight it would appear that the decision that the children had been neglected and not physically abused deflected the focus of work away from child protection where it should have been. Instead it moved on to efforts to increase the parenting skills of the adults without a sufficiently careful assessment of the care that the children received.

Including the wider family

Careful consideration needs to be given to who to include in the assessment, and who to see. In the Doreen Aston case social workers were involved with Doreen and Christine, and in a different borough with her extended family. It is noticeable that despite a serious incident between Christine and Doreen and then Christine and her sister at which her mother was present no attempt was made to understand the context of the extended family within which all this was taking place. (DA 2.175)

The Beckford inquiry notes the lack of any approach by Social Services, over three years of contact with the Beckford's with the extended family, despite the fact that the social worker had been told by Beckford that Beverly and the children were actually staying with maternal grandparents. It identifies the extended family as a source of information and possible support. (JB 85)

Parent and child involvement

The Tyra Henry inquiry makes the point 'It may sound absurd to talk now about involving Andrew Neil in planning for Tyra's wellbeing. The true starting point was not that he was a violent young man who had if possible to be kept away from Tyra. It was that he was Tyra Henry's father and, when not in custody, the regular boyfriend and near neighbour of Tyra's mother. But the preferable purpose, and in our view a feasible one, was to try to involve Andrew Neil constructively in appreciating why Tyra was having to be cared for in a particular way and in at least passively co-operating with the plan. It would have fulfilled a necessary function, which common fairness requires, that the father of a child should be told why he cannot play any part in her upbringing. It would have performed the task which instead was invidiously left to Claudette and Beatrice Henry of warning Andrew Neil off. And it would have given social services a much more precise appreciation of the nature of the problem Andrew Neil now presented'. (TH 7.5)

There are important benefits to careful consideration of who to involve in an assessment. Such involvement might not only increase information, but reduce alienation and resistance, and provide a resource. The Cleveland inquiry notes that 'the lack of basic understanding of the unique features of each family as a family meant that parents felt alienated by what they saw as an apparent lack of willingness to understand their point of view. . . . We would suggest that the gathering of knowledge upon which to place carefully considered judgements, together with cautious use of professional authority and statutory powers, are more likely to be in the best interests of vulnerable children than patterns of professional practice which alienate parents and isolate children at the centre of conflict. (CLV 4.159)

Divergence of views

The previous analysis of inquiry reports noted that perhaps the most difficult part of the assessment is the interpretation of information collected and the weighting of the various factors. It cited the minority report on the Marie Colwell case. In the 1980s the two reports into the death of Lucy Gates – the Chairman's and the panel's – illustrate the same point. There is a straight divergence of view about the interpretation of Linda Gates behaviour, and the appropriateness of the professional agencies response to it. Inquiries may allow themselves two decisions. Children in need of protection and care need one.

4.5 INTERVENTION AND PLANNING
(see also 3.2 Case Conferences)

Intervention in cases of child abuse or suspected child abuse must have a purpose. This purpose needs definition on receipt of referral, and, as more often described in the inquiries when cases are transferred, their legal status changes, and new information is received. Whilst the child protection process is normally formulated as investigation leading to assessment leading to planned treatment, in long term cases the need is to recognise 'referral' information, be able to stand back and reassess, and revise plans of action.

In order to deal with new information, and the power and turbulence of families, clarity of purpose must come first and embrace specific tasks and action.

The inquiries say a great deal about planning and decision making. They are clearer about the decisions that were made and ought to have been made, than about who should have made them. For example 'although it was agreed that the Social Services Department would write to Christine requiring her to attend the clinic with Doreen, no formal request from the case conference (sic) went to the health authority with a clear expectation that a report would be provided for its next review'. (DA 6.42)

The need for planning and decision making can take place on individual initiative or whim, for example the decision to return eight children to their mother after thirteen months in care 'seems to have been taken by social worker 1 on her own initiative'. (LGC 6.13) And again, the social worker in the Tyra Henry case recorded that neither she nor the health visitor had any worries about Tyra's care at present so they would reduce the frequency of supervision. The decision was taken without reference back to the case conference soon after the making of a care order. (TH 3.31)

Lack of planning

A lack of planning can be a recipe for drift. 'The health visitor's view of the Carlile family changed following a hostile reception she received from Mr Hall in a telephone call conversation of 14th April. She was clear in her own mind that the Carlile's were no longer willing to seek and receive help over Kimberley. But instead of turning to positive action, she became infected with the occupational disease of drift and inaction, prepared by Mr Hall's hostility. She told us that she was upset by Mr Hall . . . The idea of visiting the Carlile's was 'the sort of event that you would put off for a day when you are feeling particularly strong and able to cope with it' such natural feelings are the ingredients of drift.' (KC 123)

A statement of purpose

The Beckford inquiry notes 'had the objectives and purposes, generally and specifically, been spelled out clearly in the records it would have been immeasurably easier to determine to what extent those objectives and purposes had been achieved, and consequently to know what the next step in the process of rehabilitation should be. . . . The absence of declared objectives and purposes throughout the period of April 1982 to July 1984, together with the general skimpiness of any relevant information because of ineffective visits to the house during the last six months of Jasmine's life, makes it tolerably clear that nothing then could have deflected the social workers from an increasingly misplaced optimism about the Beckford family and a devaluation of the care orders'. (JB 225)

The purposes must be established. The Carlile inquiry describing the failure to invite health staff to case conferences notes 'the earlier concern about Kimberley's development and lack of follow up of her doubtful hearing and physical development had vanished from the social workers minds. The sole focus of their considerations was the future of the three children collectively . . . ' (KC 51-54) In the Tyra Henry case the case conference noted no reason to be concerned about the care of Tyra but 'this was based entirely on Tyra's developments as far as it had been possible to monitor it in the absence of the necessary clinic visits; it had nothing to do with the reason why Tyra was in care which was that her father might injure or kill her if he got near her'. (TH 244) The Emma Jane Hughes inquiry notes efforts being given to Mrs Hughes to provide much needed support for carrying out her responsibilities as a single parent 'however, a greater clarity in the planning of Mrs Hughes involvement in the care and control of her children with the day foster mother might have led at this stage to a clearer assessment as to whether Mrs Hughes was able to care for her own children'. (EJH 2.1.14)

Visits

The inquiries bear eloquent testimony to the need to visit, but purposeless visiting is not in itself enough: 'surveillance and supervision alone do not usually protect children from further abuse'. (KMcG 78) In Shirley Woodcock's case more frequent visiting should have been made to the foster home but the inquiry notes this should not conceal the overriding importance of undertaking the work necessary to make and implement plans to promote the welfare of the children. (SW 9.27) The guardian in the Beckford case reported 'I'm very concerned about workers going into families where the visiting is unfocused and where they are not clear, and the families are not clear, what the purpose in that particular visit is'. (JB)

The child as the focus

A purposeless visit can be part of a wider problem, failure to focus on the child. On the last sighting of Jasmine Beckford by a social worker she was recovering from a fracture of her thigh and would have walked with an abnormal gait 'If Miss Wahlstrom had carried out only the elementary task of walking with Jasmine, or talking to her, even in her mother's presence, the fact of child abuse would have been all too apparent'. (JB 126)

A plan with success criteria

It is important to establish criteria in order to judge success or failure. The Emma Jane Hughes inquiry notes that in a case review following reception into care 'The more important issues concerning how work towards rehabilitation could effectively be undertaken and what might constitute 'a change in mother's circumstances' . . . were not spelt out, nor apparently given any due importance'. (EJH 2.1.25) An unpublished report notes that within the context of evidence of considerable effort to co-ordinate activities and surveillance between the involved agencies, it was not clear to what extent there was a commonly determined plan of action to which the agency was subscribing. Observations made by the various agencies seemed mostly to be characterised by being of an impressionistic nature, with little or no attempt to establish objective criteria against which . . . progress and development could be measured.

And success can be missed: 'The (case) conference made no plans in relation to the care and protection of Doreen. As it transpired the following month the Southwark social worker had one of her most successful interviews with Christine and observation of Doreen. Unfortunately it was isolated and not followed up by her. The lack of a coherent inter-agency plan provided her with no structure for her work.' (DA 8.12)

Adequate and objective information

Had information about Andrew Neil been available before Tyra Henry was born . . . 'it would thus have cast a crucially different light on the story that Tyrone had fallen off the bed and out of a bath, and prompted intervention at a time early enough to have possibly saved him from being maimed'. (TH 2.28)

Information needs to be based in fact, subjective 'feelings', 'concerns', and 'worries' are not enough. (LJ 3.92) There needs to be clear separation of fact and opinion. In the Tyra Henry case there was expressed a view that Tyra was probably then safe because Tyrone had been a very young and difficult baby when Andrew injured him. (TH 4.31)

Information sources

Information needs to be drawn from all available sources, including expert sources such as legal advisors. (TH 4.4) The Aston and Johnson inquiries emphasise the need for full information being provided to case conferences 'case conferences are still used far too much for discussion and not enough for analysis . . . the information often seems to be given in a generalised way and it is particularly vague as the dates when incidents happened. We think that if the practice developed of agencies submitting written summaries, including the dates of any contacts with the family prior to the conference to the person chairing it, this could be collated into a chronology which would form an accurate and sensible basis for analysis and discussion'. (LJ 6.15)

Having drawn information from all sources, including extended family and neighbours the chairman should provide information on previous social worker involvement, the results of previous case conferences and details of previous injuries, if these have not already been included in medical or social worker reports. (KMcG 76) This inquiry emphasises the need for full sharing of data between agencies which can lead to joint planning. All the expert witnesses to the Cleveland inquiry agreed that intervention should proceed as planned and co-ordinated activity between agencies. (CLV 4.3) And full information is required not only for planning, per se, but also 'those responsible for the allocation of resources should be in possession of all the relevant information necessary to properly apply any relevant criteria'. (RC 98)

Case history

The Aston inquiry also emphasises the need to produce written case history for initial case conferences, to be updated for later review case conferences, and to produce a child protection plan for discussion at the case conference or as soon as possible thereafter if it is held in an emergency. (DA 6.29)

Timing

The Emma Jane Hughes inquiry sums up 'All staff working in child care cases must have a sense of urgency about the pressures of planning . . . at the same time we believe that careful consideration and presentation of the situation under review is equally vital . . . maintaining the balance is difficult and depends on a sound understanding of each others constraints and an accurate assessment of the realities faced by all at the time of the review. What is clear is that at the end of the day the decision must be taken consistent with the needs of the children and acted upon with the urgency appropriate to the needs identified'. (EJH 2.4.15)

Pre-birth planning

Tyrone Henry had been seriously injured, Claudette and Neil appeared to have split up. Claudette was pregnant with Tyra. A case conference decision was that 'once necessary forms had been completed with Claudette no further useful social work function can be offered . . . it will be up to Claudette, who is in a difficult situation, to ensure that her baby is protected from Andrew Neil'. The inquiry comments 'we think that the seeds of the tragedy had been sown before Tyra was born – not in an abstract of fatalistic sense but in that avoidable errors had by then been made which left the baby exposed to a known risk'. (TH 2.27)

Pre-birth conferences

The Aston inquiry recommends that the Department Of Health issues guidelines to the effect that authorities should consider holding case conferences in respect of unborn children, where the risk to that child may be such as to indicate the need to develop a child protection plan before birth. The inquiry believes that if a pre-birth conference had been held it might have given greater weight to the importance of making plans before birth. It might also have considered whether it was realistic to expect an assessment to be carried out while Doreen was in hospital. It would have avoided delays after birth which added to the difficulties of the presentation both to the court and to Christine and Roy. (DA 6.7-11 & 22 also LAC 90.8 and HN 90.15)

Following the initial case conference

Inquiries note the importance of timely decisions. 'If the initial case conference had decided that a child protection plan should be produced as soon as possible after the conference, this would have provided a structure for the social worker and a document on which future discussions should have been based. The plan should have been discussed with Christine and Roy (Aston) and could have included: a statement of the reasons why the Social Services were concerned; a statement about expectations of involvement of the social worker with the family eg. to obtain access to undertake a comprehensive assessment; a statement of the inter-linking roles of each profession; a statement about the consequences if Christine and Roy did not co-operate with the Social Services eg. a discussion of legal proceedings . . . In conjunction with the minutes . . . this would have been available to all future case conferences. If the terms of the plan had not been adhered to it would be obvious to all and it would also be easy for agencies to take up the matter with senior management of another agency if they felt that that agency was not carrying out its agreed function.' (DA 6.26)

Once a statutory order has been made

The Beckford inquiry emphasised the need for a case conference after a court decision to take stock of information gathered through the court process (see above). Careful planning of the management of a supervision order is important too. In relation to Karl McGoldrick who was made subject to a supervision order the inquiry refers to the need for a plan to be inforce for monitoring care to be undertaken by a core team involving health visitor, social worker and possibly the child's school. At the very least planning would ensure that all involved knew that the supervision order was in force – the health visitor in this case had never been made formally aware of this. (KMcG 55 & KMcG 38)

Prior to placement

The need is particularly great to review and plan when consideration is being given to a child going home on trial and prior to foster placement. 'A decision to return a child to the family must always be the prime, positive ingredient in any planned process to reunite the family, and not merely the consequence of returned to the parents their child. It must include a protection plan.' (JB 124) The inquiry recommends that whenever a child, who has been abused by its parents, is returned to its family home on trial there must be a protection plan, to which the parents must be contractually bound. Its contractual element should be regular visits to see (and talk to) the children on their own; regular medical examination at the clinic; nursery or school attendance depending upon the age of the child; a requirement to notify the local authority if the child is to stay away from home overnight. Such planning, to which the parent should be bound is an essential expression of the fact that the child remains 'in trust' to the local authority. (JB 115 & 289)

Means to an end

Some inquiries consider that child abuse registration can provide an appropriate focus for planning and case management. (JB 120 & KMcG 60) On the other hand recognition is given to the fact that child abuse procedures are not ends in themselves. The Liam Johnson inquiry is concerned 'that in some quarters having a case conference is regarded as the solution to a difficult problem rather than a forum for discussion and analysis. We think is may also be used as a substitute by other agencies for taking action which properly belongs to them'. (LJ 6.13) The Aston inquiry makes the point that a forthcoming case conference should not inhibit action being taken when it is needed. (DA 6.53 also HK 1.25)

Consideration of alternatives

Planning and decision making require all alternatives in pursuit of the purposes and objectives, should be considered. This should include consideration of alternative courses of legal action. (DA 7.12 & KMcG 53)

Considering alternatives can improve objectivity (CLV 4.51) particularly in relation to decisions to move children to and from their homes in which professionals attitudes to residential care, often pessimistic, may affect their judgement. The Jasmine Beckford inquiry took the view expressed by BAAF that 'so long as coming into residential care is part of a considered plan for the long term care of the child, then it may be the best thing that could be done'. (JB 263)

Absence of alternatives

The absence of alternatives actually being available is referred to in the inquiries, as has been noted above. Clearly, alternatives need to related to available resources, but the process of analysis, the consideration of alternatives in relation to stated objectives, so that objectives can be tested, is an essential part of planning.

Long term and short term planning

Alternatives need to be considered in terms of their short and long term consequences. Consideration of the use of respite care for the Gates children, in the view of the Chairman's inquiry served 'to emphasise how temporary solutions, by relieving the pressure, delay and distort the decision making process'. (LGC 38.7) In that context no clear assessment of risk took place bringing together all information, and the inquiry notes the absence for co-ordinated long term plan. (LGC 35.11)

Planning should also involve planning for contingencies, for example, in the event of an unsuccessful care application, or dealing with a highly mobile family which may involve rapid transfer of the case. (DA 6.29)

Ambiguous decisions

The Tyra Henry inquiry notes that the case conference had two alternatives regarding Tyra's safety one, for the local authority to assume responsibility and the other for Beatrice Henry to do so. 'The vice of the course decided on, leaving aside at the moment its ambiguous formulation, was that it tried to follow both routes at once: it accepted council responsibility for Tyra but sought to discharge it by delegating it wholesale to Beatrice Henry. . . . The result that the council was going to be in no position directly to fulfil its own mandate to protect the child, and that Beatrice Henry was going to be coping on the council's behalf . . . Indeed the decision made Beatrice Henry's position almost impossible, because if danger arose and she went to social services to warn them, the result might well be that Tyra was taken away from both Claudette and herself. Even allowing for hindsight, we are struck by the failure to see the inherent contradictions and risks of the arrangements.' (TH 3.10)

'Drift'

Inquiries also demonstrate how decisions can 'drift'. In the absence of the minutes of a conference the Aston inquiry saw three versions of plans agreed at a case conference. (DA 6.28) Significant drifting took place in the decision about the care of Tyra Henry. 'Without any discernal proposal or conscious discussion or decision, and in breach of the basis on which the magistrates had granted Lambeth the order, the case conference took the responsibility for Tyra out of her grandmother's hands and silently placed it in her mother's.' (TH 4.12)

Response to new information: reappraisal of purpose

There is a need for workers to be responsive to new information and be prepared to reassess and reappraise, particularly in long term cases where workers may individually or together become set in their views. 'At no time after April 1982 was Jasmine weighed . . . failure to take particular note of Jasmine's weight over the three years of the care order is perhaps the most striking, single aspect of child abuse that was fatally neglected. This is a failure which social workers and health visitors must alike share the blame. Social workers may refer to the child's weight, but we gain the impression that rarely do they draw the proper inferences from it when monitoring cases of child abuse. We suspect that this is true of some health visitors, and even doctors.' (JB 114)

The chair of a case conference is important in generating reappraisal. 'Although we appreciate (he) was dependent on the actions of the other agencies involved and on the information made available to him by these agencies, little attempt seems to have been made to question or analyze these actions or to review the information critically, objectively, and in depth. Everything seems to have been accepted at face value.' (KMcG 60)

The danger is that case conference decisions, when made, are regarded as inviolable. (KMcG 40) The Richard Fraser inquiry makes a similar point: '(the) plan was to help Richard by giving support and guidance to his family in the hope that family life would improve and so bring benefit to the child. In this, a leading role was played by Social Services, which followed generally all the procedures laid down. But we feel that the management plan was adhered to with too much rigidity . . . far more attention was given at times to the family as a whole than to Richard as an individual. There were several times where the opportunity could have been taken to remove Richard from home, or to make an assessment of him, but no one was pursued'. (RF 136)

Lack of reappraisal

Failure to assess new information, reappraisal, is not a problem solely related to case conferences 'we gain the impression that over the years the principle medical officer developed an acceptance of Miss Gates as a mother with multiple problems who would not deliberately injure her children. Much of the information received by (her) should have led to this doctor adopting a more authoritative approach. We would have anticipated greater initiative by (her) in the management of attempts to resolve the failure of Lucy to thrive'. (LGP 5.39)

The need to review objectives is well illustrated by the Lucy Gates case. 'In achieving the chosen policy of keeping the children united with their mother: the boy had spent just over one third of his life with nine different foster parents and twelve placements. The older girl has spent approximately one half of her life with eight different foster parents and ten placements. In addition during the time that the three children were in their mother's care the boy had eight admissions to hospital, the elder girl three and Lucy seven. The children were also cared for away from the family household sometimes overnight and sometimes longer periods by friends, neighbours and a relative.' (LGP 1.7)

There is a need to gather information over reasonable periods of time, and not make decisions on the basis of scant observation or single sightings. What is clear from the inquiries, though, is that judgement made early in cases can have long term consequences if new information is not let in.

Review conferences

The value of a review process in bringing to light deficient implementation of previous case conference recommendations is repeatedly noted. (KMcG 60 TH 7.14 EJH 2.4.59 KC 1.66)

Implementation of decisions

It is essential that once decisions have been made they are implemented. 'One recommendation was that for Beverly to be encouraged to attend clinic monthly and health visitor to visit about fortnightly. Since no health visitor was present, and no communication seems to have been made, it is not surprising this became a dead letter.' (JB 110) 'There is no record that Avon Palethorpe or anyone else conveyed to the housing department, the decision that Claudette was not to be rehoused on her own.' (TH 3.22) Plans need to be resourceable. 'Plans were made for Christine to go to a family centre with her baby and with the man thought to be the father. Because of Christine's variable commitment and a long wait for a place, they had not been achieved by the time of the child's death.' (DA 2.6) Plans should be adhered to with commitment. Note for example two entries in case conference minutes relating to Tyra Henry '(the social worker) said she had never felt that Claudette would hurt Tyra and did not consider that the child was at risk. She never felt that committed to the care order on Tyra because the situation had changed considerably by the time it was made. However, the court would probably not agree to its discharge at present'. And later in the minutes 'Many of the decisions at the last conference have still yet to be carried out and therefore have been included in the recommendations below'. (TH 4.23)

The previous study of inquiry reports made the point that the authority to intervene between parents and their children is rooted in law and in powers which derive from decisions of the court and reviewed social workers use of authority, or failure to use it in relation to families. In this report discussions of the relationship between parents, families and the use of the law is broadened (see above). This report here considers a number of aspects of the use of the law and the court process in relation to investigation assessment and planning.

Quality of legal advice

In order to use the law there needs to be sound knowledge of it. A number of inquiries emphasise the need for professionals in many agencies in particular social workers, to be adequately trained in this respect. A number of inquiries emphasised the need for good legal advice. This most strongly put in the Beckford inquiry. Additionally there is a clearly stated need for legal advisors to attend case conferences, in particular initial case conferences to advise on conditions that need to be fulfilled for an application for an order; powers or conditions that a specific court order would provide a local authority; the appropriateness for particular order in a particular case. (KMcG 77, CLV 4.28, JC 3.4.38, TH 6.17) There is a need to formalise the relationship of consultation between social workers and legal advisors. Guidelines need to be available to social workers or anyone else on how to instruct the legal department. Such guidelines need to include directions as to written material provided to the legal department and the circumstances in which advice may be given orally or in writing. It should be a minimum expectation that whatever the instructions, the solicitor should ensure that s/he is in possession of all the facts so that adequate legal advice can be given. (DA 3.36 and 7.12-18)

Court hearings are part of a planning process

Court applications should be viewed as an integral part of the planning process for the child. Preparation of the case for the juvenile court and care proceedings should be regarded not as a burden or formality but a significant opportunity for the local authority to assemble and critically review its own proposals. Correspondingly, both lawyers and the court should be concerned to probe the viability of what is proposed and if necessary must be prepared to send the plan back to the drawing board. (TH 6.5)

Systematic consideration of legal options sharpens awareness of the reality of the choice that was being made (for example TH 11.1 and DA 7.12). The Cleveland inquiry makes the point that 'during the period of the crisis particularly when the dispute over medical evidence became known objective legal advice on the probabilities of the outcome of each case would have been invaluable and the seeking of it prudent'. (CLV 10.32)

When a care order is made it is important to review all the information that has been gathered during the court process and consideration given to how that information affects the execution of statutory duties to the child in their care. Preparing and giving evidence is an important discipline to assist reaching clear judgements and decisions; the value is, of course, lost to those who prejudge what the court's findings would be. In the context of a care application which resulted in the making of a supervision or rather than a care order an unpublished inquiry emphasises the need for contingency planning before (rather than after) the hearing. And is essential that if issues in a case are to be fully explored by the courts, of proceedings to be brought at all, that evidence is properly collected.

The problem of delay in court hearings

A number of inquiries expressed concern about delays in court hearings, both in terms of getting to a final hearing in the juvenile court due to congestion in the juvenile court system (for example JB 30), and more often in these inquiries, delays in adult prosecutions. The Beckford inquiry strongly recommends that in future in child abuse prosecutions involving children in the care of the local authority where the public is almost certain to express concern about the handling of the case by Social Services or other relevant agencies, criminal trials should other than for exceptional reasons take place within 3-4 months of homicidal incident, and certainly not beyond six months. This recommendation is extended to include children not in the care of the local authority who die in circumstances of concern, in the Carlile report. (JB KC)

The Liam Johnson inquiry notes problems of co-ordination between the adult court hearing and court proceedings in respect of the child. In that case the discretionary power to supervise access, imposed in wardship, was turned into an obligation to do so by one of the father's bail conditions causing considerable management problems for the Social Services Department. It considers that 'the court system is not a cohesive whole and that the left hand of the court system does not know what the right hand is doing'. The Doreen Aston inquiry notes the need for substantial improvements in court process with the implementation of the Children Act 1989. The court system will need to be responsive to emergency intervention both in terms of the availability of court time for an early hearing and in terms of understanding the planning processes for the child. (DA 731)

Clarity of role in court

In recent years there has been an increase in the number of care proceedings and they are now frequently strongly contested in an atmosphere which could be hostile to the local authority social worker. (SW 8) Clarity of role is essential. Legal support will be needed for the preparation of the case; the social workers should concentrate on what is more properly their function. Court proceedings can place the relationship of professionals severely at risk so that as much clarity of role as possible between professionals and parents is essential. An unpublished report examines in detail the process of a court hearing. Social workers fulfil two roles – giving factual evidence and expert evidence. It is essential that the case is presented to make the quality and status of social workers' evidence clear and strong.

The role of solicitors in court hearings is considered by a number of enquiries. The Richard Fraser inquiry expresses concern that the local authority solicitor made an arrangement with the family solicitor without informing the social worker, who felt after the event that the solicitors advice, about a care order and Richard going home on trial, had to be accepted. (RF 58) The Beckford inquiry describes role comparison in the child's solicitor between the needs of the parents and the children. He did not see the children and the inquiry recommends that 'any solicitor acting for children in care proceedings must see, and if possible talk to or play with, those whose interests he is hired to protect and promote'. (JB 103) The Lucy Gates inquiry, also emphasised that the presentation of the case is a matter for a solicitor who is familiar with the work or Social Services and who is well versed in the law relating to child care and conversant with the evidential problems likely to be encountered. (LGC 42.2)

Court officers

A number of inquiries comment on the role of the court liaison officer. The Cleveland inquiry notes that none of the court liaison officers were qualified either as a barrister or a solicitor. The Beckford inquiry discusses the role of court officers and considers that legal departments of local authorities should arrange for one or more of their solicitors to specialise in juvenile court work. Relating to the role of the court officer it notes there a number of tasks in which the local authority assist the juvenile court where legal training is not necessary: preparing and presenting social inquiry reports; making arrangements for the placement of juveniles on remand or an interim order; to note requests emerging from the bench; in the absence of a parent or guardian to act as local friends and sit beside the juvenile in court; to provide a link with other local authorities in relation to juveniles from other areas. (JB 259-261)

Guardian ad litem

Inquiries highlight the value of the guardian ad litem in care proceedings. The essential feature of that role is for the first time there is someone, other than a legal representative whose is concerned exclusively with the welfare of the child, independent of both the child's parents and of the local authority which has the duty to protect the child. The Beckford inquiry recommends extensive use of the guardian. (JB 253) Guardians need to act objectively and critically in relation to the role of the local authority in relation to the child. (KMcG 64) A guardian should have access to all reports and case records regarding the child and family, and whenever possible interview all medical and character referees. Whilst the guardians role is solely to report to the court and additional recommendations made have no legal basis, they are an added source of expertise any additional recommendations they might make should, at the discretion of the court, be circulated to the various agencies involved. (KMcG 80) The Cleveland inquiry emphasises that the independence of the guardian must be demonstrated and commends arrangements in Cleveland to do so, and it recommends that amendment is needed to the relevant rules to define more closely the role of the guardian. This work in relation to guardians has been taken forward in the Children Act 1989.

Magistrates and judges

Some inquiries consider the role of magistrates. The Beckford inquiry considers this most closely, following the magistrates' rider to the parents that 'the Social Services will do everything to help you both and get your children back to you'. The inquiry considers that the juvenile court magistrates do not have jurisdiction to add riders in these circumstances. It is essential that in care proceedings at least, a magistrate should be required to give full and adequate reasons relating to the care and supervision of the children.

The inquiry looks forward to the establishment of a family court comprising highly professional juvenile magistrates. 'It is a lack of training and understanding among many magistrates . . . that has lead legal practitioners and other observers to express unhappiness that the quality of justice meted out to children, to parents and local authorities in care proceedings.' (JB 167) The Cleveland inquiry also refers to the establishment of a family court recognising the considerable procedural advantages of having the ability to move cases at any time from one tier of the court to another which would be achieved by setting up of a family court. (CL 253)

Place of safety orders and emergency protection

The use of place of safety orders is discussed in a number of reports, most particularly in the Cleveland inquiry report. The inquiry notes that an instruction from the Director of Social Services that 'where the consultant paediatrician is of the opinion that there is medical evidence of sexual abuse, an immediate place of safety should be taken to protect the child's interest during the investigation' led to a 'pre-emptory use of authority which alienated parents and made the proper task of social workers impractical that is to say the carrying out of a full assessment of the family'. (CLV 4.186) It notes additionally the problems of using hospitals as a place of safety for children most of whom had no medical problem requiring nursing or medical attention. The inquiry recommends that place of safety orders should only be sought for the minimum time necessary to ensure protection of the child. Records related to the use of statutory powers on a emergency basis should be kept and monitored by the Social Services Departments. And the code of practice for the administration by social workers or emergency orders for the purposes of child protection including a provision of information to parents to finding their rights in clear simple language should be drawn up. (CLV 246)

The Doreen Aston inquiry considers a different point in relation to a place of safety orders. Considering a dispute between adjacent level of authority as to which should take responsibility for application, it recommends the guidance is issued to Director of Social Services the responsibility for action in relation to a place of safety order lies with the authority where the child is found at the time of the incident. If the child is in care or on the child abuse register only if that authority is prepared to accept responsibility is the first authority absolved from responsibility. (DA 2.176)

The Charlene Salt inquiry was concerned about place of safety orders lapsing. It expressed the need that no place of safety order should be allowed to lapse without authority from a senior officer.

The Doreen Aston inquiry considers emergency protection orders under the Children Act 1989. 'The requirement that a protection order will only be granted where there is a real emergency means that local authorities will have to give more frequent consideration to taking proceedings when a child is still at home. The practice of looking for an incident which would justify removal should in the future be unacceptable. 'Proper assessment should be the basis for proceedings. In particular given the criteria of the likelihood of significant harm, authorities will have to use the courts as part of planned intervention rather than as a response to crisis.' (DA 7.31) 'It will be essential for the courts, those providing evidence to the courts, and those commenting on the performance of those working in this field to give careful consideration to the methods of demonstrating in evidence that there is a likelihood of significant harm.' (DA 7.32)

Use of warrants

A number of inquiries consider social workers understanding and use of warrants to search for a child or young person. The Heidi Koseda inquiry recommended changes to CYPA 1933 (40). The Kimberley Carlile inquiry recommended 'a bunch of orders' relating to both to the investigation of cases of child abuse and to immediate action and where child abuse is suspected, that is: a power to enter and inspect the premises where a child is living and is thought to be at risk, coupled with the right to see the child; a child assessment order for the protection of the child and medical examination; a warrant to search for or remove the child an emergency protection order; and a police officer's right of entering without a search warrant.

Voluntary care?

The Emma Jane Hughes inquiry notes, in the context of the considerations to take care proceedings rather than to allow the continuation of successive receptions into care, 'the emphasis placed by the social worker and the senior social worker on the value which they ascribe to the voluntary co-operation between the social worker and Mrs Hughes. When the children were in care the social worker found herself having to negotiate to keep them there and therefore the situation was being dictated by Mrs Hughes rather than the social worker in the best interests of the children'. (EJH 2.1.17)

A number of inquiries describe sequences of voluntary reception into care contributing to drift and lack of planning in the case, and the lack of thorough assessment of the needs of the children therein (for example LGP 3.59).

Failures to use the law

There are numerous incidence of failures to exercise legal authorities held, and there are instances of inadequate supervision where there is an order is in force. Most common are breaches of Boarding Out Regulations, which set out minimum standards of the frequency of visits, medical examinations and reviews (for example SW 5.0, LGP 5.81, 'A' 5, JB 25). The Cleveland case inquiry noted that children were not examined in accordance with Boarding Out Regulations in time of their placement at the foster home. The result was that there was uncertainty as to their medical condition at the moment of placement with the foster parents and whether or not there was any change afterwards. (CLV 4.133) The Shirley Woodcock summary quotes the Department of Health and Social Security Social Work Service Report (A study of the boarding out regulations July 1981) which records 'widespread disregard of the Boarding Out Children Regulations'. The Tyra Henry inquiry notes how imaginative use of boarding out arrangements could have greatly benefitted Tyra Henry's mother 'as it represented a form of arrangement governed by statutory regulations and supported by a substantial weekly cash payment which is disregarded . . . in assessing the foster parents eligibility in supplementary benefit'. (TH 11.3-11.6)

The Government has now introduced revised Boarding Out Regulations and in addition regulations relating to children 'home on trial' (Charge and Control Regulations). In the light of lessons to be learned from these inquiries regulations relating to 'home on trial' are an important step forward. They need to be implemented.

Law reform

A number of inquiries comment on specific aspects of law reform, as referred to above, as part of the consultation process on child care law reform. It is essential to recognise the new demands which have been made by the Children Act and for local authority to take note of the major resource implications which will result from the Act, and ensure that in the light of these implications is able to fulfil its statutory duties in relation to child protection. ('A' 39)

Thousands of children enjoy the care of foster parents who play a unique and special role in their lives. Three of the child abuse inquiries relate to children who died in foster care, one to a child dying in a pre adoption placement and one inquiry is about sexual abuse within a foster home.

Most references to fostering in the inquies relate to the happy experience of children later killed at home, in foster care earlier in their lives. In the latter context four themes run through the inquiries; the need for foster care to be purposeful; the need to obtain information before during and after the placement to enable a judgement to be made about the quality of care at home (JB 114 for example); the need to take the opportunity of using foster care as a forum within which assessment of the children can take place; and the need to engage in planned work with the parents whilst the children are in care (for example LGC 37.71 and SW 4.30).

Selection of foster homes

The importance of thorough assessment during the selection process is emphasised. The Emma Jane Hughes inquiry notes that the process for approving Mr and Mrs Danielson's application to become foster parents was generally conducted with a low level of professional practice and the adequacy of supervision given to the social worker was questionable. (EJH 7.7.2) The Shirley Woodcock report expresses serious reservations about the decision to approve as foster parents. (SW 2.24 also EJH 22.9)

Acknowledging abuse in selection process

A thorough assessment provides a bench line against which to judge any subsequent allegations of abuse. The Cleveland inquiry notes that following admission into care of children from foster homes that 'the fact that foster parents have been through a selection process which would have involved making careful inquiries into their background and the taking up of references does not seem to have weighed the social workers in deciding how they should respond to the medical opinions expressed by the consultant paediatricians involved. As a result, children whose lives have already suffered disruption were moved again without any preparation'. (CLV 4.135) This is all the more valuable if abuse is acknowledged and discussed in the selection process. The inquiry into Mr and Mrs 'A' emphasises that foster parents should understand the nature of social workers responsibility for foster children, which involves allowing for the possibility that any foster parent may be an abuser. ('A' 6)

Problems of rapid placement

The inquiries note the problems which follow rapid placement. The Cleveland inquiry notes the use of newly approved foster parents with complicated cases with inadequate preparations; and taking advantage of kind-heartedness of foster parents and placing more children than they could cope with, and the impossibility of giving any real thought and matching the needs of the child with what a foster family had to offer. (CLV 4.69)

Rushing placement may lead to a lack of understanding of what is involved in fostering and a failure to appreciate the importance of foster parents working in partnership with social services. (JB 109) Both Jason Plischkowsky and Shirley Woodcock were placed in haste – Shirley without previously meeting the foster parents. (JP 10 and SW 1.60) The Christopher Pinder inquiry considers the very short timescale between the approval of the Franklands and the placement of children with them. (CP/DF 7.2) And the Mr and Mrs 'A' inquiry refers, in relation to placement to unacceptable 'short cuts' being taken by the Department. ('A' 4)

One of the consequences of rapid placement, and short cuts, can be that the placement of children does not follow conditions which may have been set down at the time of the approval. The Shirley Woodcock inquiry discussed unclear authority in relation to these conditions. It recommended that a fostering panel should be given authority as the only decision making body for approval and registration of foster parents, matching of children to a long term basis to foster parents, and proposed changes of usage of foster parents. Any observations made by the panel which define the type of child to be placed should be regarded as restrictions on the usage of the placement and should be made known in full to the placing social worker. (SW 4.16) Both the Emma Jane Hughes inquiry and the Beckford inquiry note problems of definition of length of stay at foster parents and the unprecise use of terminology such as 'short term'. They recommended standardisation of terms. (EJH 3.2.2 and JB 80)

Short term placements

Inquiries note the strain of short placements. When a child needs an urgent placement 'it may sometimes be desirable for a temporary residential placement to be made, so that the process of finding suitable foster parents, and preparing them to meet the needs of the child can be carried out more carefully'. (JB 271)

The Shirley Woodcock inquiry notes that the Boarding Out Regulations refer to 'short' and 'long term' placements. The foster homes used for Shirley and her brother were designated short term but staff in Social Services referred to such a placement as 'interim' or 'open ended' i.e. neither short term nor long term. The report notes the stress on foster parents of the extension of short stay placements which might involve considerable contact with the child's family, attending court and giving evidence, and dealing with children who may exhibit behaviour problems. (SW 4.22)

Support for foster parents

Inquiries express concern about the social work input and support to foster parents during placement. The Emma Jane Hughes inquiries record the feelings of officers interviewed who regarded the level of support given to foster parents was in need of improvement and should be given higher priority than was presently the case. (EJH 3.3.2) The 'A' inquiry recommends a more probing intervention that simply support. Intervention must include sensitive but probing discussion of difficult personal topics; there must be explicit review of the foster family whose structure has changed and this review should be undertaken as a matter of high priority. ('A' R7)

Boarding Out Regulations to be followed

Boarding Out Regulations were often not followed. (JP 2.5 & EJH 7.3.6) In the Shirley Woodcock case where Boarding Out Regulations were disregarded in many respects. The inquiry summary quotes Department Of Health and Social Security Social Work Service Report based on a national study of practice of Social Services Department: 'There was widespread disregard of the Boarding-Out of Children Regulations ... Although needed amendment in some respects, the Boarding-Out Regulations have withstood the passing of time remarkably well as a framework of practice. Although apparently detailed, they prescribe only minimum standards to safeguard a vulnerable group of children, but even these minimum standards were neglected and some in places, seemed unknown'. (SW 5.40)

The inquiry notes that Boarding Out Regulations do not apply to a foster home in which children are placed on a place of safety order. However good professional practice demands at least the same degree of support and supervision is offered to foster parents having care of the child who is subject to a place of safety order as would be given if the child were in care. More support than usual may be required in view of the recent trauma or removal. (SW 5.22) The review into Mr and Mrs 'A' records that the statutory regulations concerning visits, medical examinations and review were not met in all cases, and recommends that 'the new Boarding Out Regulations, (which impose considerably more demands on local authorities than hitherto) be followed to the letter . . . ' ('A' R3)

Trans-racial fostering

To the Beckford inquiry it appeared at the outset that exceptionally among the many recent inquiries into cases of child abuse inquiries, that there was a discrete racial dimension to the case of Jasmine Beckford (although in the end little or no part in our consideration). The placement for fostering an Afro-Caribbean child with an Anglo-Indian foster father and English foster mother provoked debate about the propriety and ethicacy to trans-racial fostering'. (JB 7) The inquiry concluded 'We do not favour any ban on trans-racial fostering. We recognise that techniques of good matching may indicate that black children in care may more often than not have a better opportunity in life if they are fostered with black families. But we stress that it is the replication of the child's cultural heritage to this prospective foster parent's cultural life that matters. Race and colour are important, but not decisive components of such matching. Each case of a black child in care must be considered on its own merits. There must be no policy laid down in advance as to where the child's best interests lie. We recommend that a greater effort be made to recruit black families as prospective foster parents in order to provide the greatest measure of choice to local authorities seeking to place for fostering and adoption of black children in their care'.
(JB 2.85)

Reduced contact with children

The Lucy Gates inquiries quotes the Chief Social Work Officer (January 1982) following inspections by his staff in Social Services Departments throughout the country. 'Children in care of these authorities who have been boarded out receive less attention than other children in care, less attention than the minimum requirements of the statutory regulations and less attention than the objective reality of their situation warranted. These omissions in the care of children arise from deficiencies in policy, management, supervision and social work practice.' (LGP 5.80) The published inquiries do not contain the same depth of information about the families where deaths occurred, as the reports into children dying at home.

The single lesson to be learned, is that child abuse takes place in foster homes, and this knowledge should affect the manner of selection, the speed of placement, and the social work contact in placement.

Blocks to recognition

In foster care there can be particular blocks to recognition. Foster parents will be keen to keep children and may have difficulty in revealing any problems being encountered. (SW 1.72) Christopher Pinder's pre adopted mother when he was seven months old, three months before his death referred to herself 'as desperate and not being able to cope with him'. She talked about 'sending him back', 'the baby was thriving but Mrs Frankland was in despair because of his screaming, demanding and changeable needs'. By the end of the interview, (with a social worker) Mr and Mrs Frankland had decided upon 'over anxiety' as the cause of their feelings and Mrs Frankland was said to have regained 'her usual efficient manner'. (CP 3.4.2) On a visit to Emma Jane Hughes Mrs Danielson pointed out bruises to Emma's head which she explained Emma had received after walking into a table. The inquiry was 'informed by both senior social worker and the social worker that at no time did they have any reason to suspect physical abuse by Mr and Mrs Danielson on Emma'. Any reservations were, 'in no way in connection with fear of physical abuse . . . but rather 'a question as to whether the Danielson's understood the fostering needs of children'. (EJH 2.4.34-35)

Continual assessment

The Shirley Woodcock report emphasises the need to assess progress in foster care. For example, when the foster mother informed fostering officer that Shirley was a 'faddy eater' early in the placement, this was the first reference to feeding difficulties. (SW 1.68) The report into Mr and Mrs 'A' recommends that in all cases foster parents are seen regularly as a family – at approval and review stages, and when possible at normal and unannounced visits. It noted that throughout the case the abuser was seldom mentioned and only ever seen by chance. In fact he had sole care of children when his wife was absent from home for too prolonged periods, and it is now known that he was sexually abusing some of the children in his care during these periods as well as when his wife was at home. ('A' 4)

'We note, too, that a number of serious difficulties in the 'A' household were apparent but not dealt with, that the social workers spent insufficient time with the children, lacking the skills in some cases to listen sensitively to them, that the concerns of other professionals about this family were regularly ignored by the Social Services Department.' ('A' 4)

It makes the important point as its first recommendation that the motivation to foster, though it may be honourable, may also be dishonourable; and that accordingly all applicants should be regarded as having a potential to abuse. ('A' R1)

Good record keeping

The inquiries regularly note problems of information giving and record keeping in relation to children in foster homes. A number of themes stand out: the problems of assembling health information after children have been taken into foster care; (JP 30 for example); the need to keep accurate information about sequences of placement in respect of children, and about what happened in placement in respect of foster parents (LGP 3.19 for example). The problems of authority and communication between fostering specialists and area social work staff (EJH 2.4.33 for example).

Every report, as did earlier reports, reveals problems in some aspect of communication between individuals and agencies. A great many communication problems are caused by confusion over roles, as described in above. To appreciate information it is necessary to be able to identify the assumptions underpinning what workers in their different roles and functions say and do.

In child protection work there are two particular challenges to good communication. The first is to develop trust. Workers share private relationships with their clients, and with their supervisors. Inter-agency working means sharing information with people who may or may not be known and trusted. Because of that there can be no substitute for building direct links and personal relationships. The second problem to develop effective communication to overcome problems inherent in communication between large numbers of people.

The Christopher Pinder inquiry sums this up well 'A feature of this case was the number of professional and non professional people who became involved with the family. The situation may have been unavoidable due to agency responsibilities and staffing difficulties, but attention is drawn to the questionable level of inter-agency communication and liaison, which led to relevant information not being shared, increased the potential for giving conflicting advice and contributed to warning signs not being interpreted'. (CP 7.3)

What ever drawbacks inter-agency liaison needs clarity of function and process because good communication requires individual workers to see their work as being interrelated with the work of others. The breakdown of communication between agencies in Cleveland was fuelled in part by a lack of understanding about other professionals legitimate involvement in cases, their role, and their points of view.

Transfer of cases

Reports comment on the need for close liaison between local authorities and Social Services Departments both when transferring cases, and when working jointly together on the same case: the Doreen Aston inquiry comments at length about responsibilities of local authorities jointly involved in a case in the taking of a place of safety order.

The Liam Johnson inquiry considers local authorities roles in transferring cases. '(The transferring-out local authority) may wish to make suggestions about the future managing of the case, how it may be dealt with by the receiving agency, or at the very least what they were planning to do had the case remained with them. It is, however for the receiving agency to make its own assessment to what action is required and to consider for example, whether a child abuse case conference should be called.' (LJ 6.4)

Changes of staff

Changes of staff pose particular challenges to good communication, and the inquiry provide examples of breakdowns of communication within and between agencies when staff changes occur. For example, the health visitor's last visit to the Beckford home before handing over the case to a successor found Jasmine 'rather a pathetic child' and 'still looked pinched'. That description never seemed to be appreciated by (the successor) when she took over and it was never referred to Social Services. (JB 118) When the Lucy Gates case was transferred, the incoming social worker said she was given no information of the previous admission to care or about the complaints and concerns which had been expressed about the children. The senior social worker and the Divisional Social Services officer said they were in the same position. (LGC)

As a team leader told the Carlile inquiry if children were coming 'from another authority to Kensington, I would have expected to have had some kind of personal contact and in the personal contact I would have hoped that they would bring the file so that we could have a look at it'. (KC 56)

Inter-agency communication

As the previous review of inquiries noted, a problem of inter-agency communication is that key words and expressions mean different things to different people. There was a misunderstanding about what was meant by 'joint investigation' (KC); 'thriving' is open to misunderstanding – does it mean a child is not failing to thrive, or that a child is doing well (DA); and there are misunderstanding about 'urgency'. Such problems are increased when procedural guidelines between agencies and between agencies and the Area Review Committee are not consistent with each other. (HK)

There can be misunderstanding about action as well as words. The Liam Johnson inquiry discussing whether or not a new partner should be told of previous violence says 'it is easy for social workers to assume that a visit from the social work services will make such a partner aware that there must be some concern. This is not necessarily so. A. thought that the Social Services always checked up when the children moved from a home in one part of the country to live with someone else'. (LF 4.13-4.15)

Confidentiality

Good communication within the inter-agency context requires that each agency has clear policies about access to information by parents and children, and clearly stated policies on confidentiality, and that these are understood by other agencies. The Richard Fraser inquiry notes 'Perhaps the Hillmead School report was written without giving the essential detail because it was thought that the parents might be able to have access to it. The paucity of real information made the report of little value to the new school'. (RF 87) 'Social worker 2 did not discuss the history of the case with the health visitors because she did not realise that they had been involved with the Gates family for any length of time. Neither did the health visitors realise that social worker 2 and her superiors were not fully conversant with the background. Social worker 2 did not ask to see their records or discuss the possible content because, in her experience, all medical records were regarded as strictly confidential.' (LGC 11.8)

The issue of confidentiality remains problematic for clients, and professionals. From the clients point of view in Samantha's story: 'I was worried in case what I told people might be told to other people. I needed to feel what I said was very secure. I could not trust many people'. (CLV 10) On the other hand in the Christopher Pinder inquiry 'There are, however, situations in child care where the concept of confidentiality becomes a barrier to communication and may place the child unnecessarily at risk. This may well have been a factor in this case'. The report emphasises that the withholding of information between professionals is 'unacceptable where non disclosure may have an influence upon the future safety of the child'. (CP 7.4)

The Cleveland inquiry quotes the recommendation of the General Medical Council in 1987 that 'if a doctor has reason for believing that a child is physically abused, not only is it permissable for the doctor to disclose information to a third party but it is the duty of the doctor to do so'. The Liam Johnson inquiry quotes this recommendation too as it is addressed in Government guidelines 'Working Together'. The inquiry sees no reason why this principle should not apply to the police.

Both the Liam Johnson and Tyra Henry inquiries examine confidentiality in relation to the police. The Tyra Henry inquiry considers the Home Office Circular (179.76) 'which stresses on the one hand the need to make all relevant convictions available to the conference, and on the other hand the importance of not revealing convictions which are not relevant'. Taking the example of Claudette Henry the inquiry 'can well see how on one view the fact that a child's mother has been charged with or convicted of shoplifting had nothing to do with the care or safety of the child. But we have pointed out above in relation to the probation service that in a less obvious sense it was a very material fact capable of radically effecting the care plan for Tyra'. The inquiry recommends 'that the Home Office's guidance to chief officers of police should recognise that the judgement of what charges or convictions are relevant to case conferences on children at risk or in care is often dependent on a wide range of factors, not all of them self-evident, and that it should advise officers to consult the person who is to chair the conference before coming to a decision against disclosure of any but the most irrelevant charges or convictions'. (TH 10.12)

The inquiry notes that the Home Office Circular also stresses the need for care in interpreting details of convictions which are given and also suggests that relevant police information other than criminal records may be conveyed on the same strict terms as conviction details.

The Liam Johnson inquiry also addresses, uniquely among the inquiries, the circumstances in which the Social Services Department ought to divulge to a new cohabitee information about violence towards a previous partner or the children of the previous relationship. It concludes that 'at the end of the day it must be a matter for the discretion of those in possession of the information', and offers guidance:

'i)   The workers should have clear in their minds the child protection issues which arise from the particular conduct. It is these which need to be addressed.

ii) The violent conduct should be raised first with the person against whom the allegations are made. He or she should then be invited to tell the new partner themselves, failing which the Social Services will do so, especially where this is the reason for concern about the current family situation.

iii) It is obviously easy to disclose allegations which are admitted to be true. Where the allegations are disputed, disclosure of the information is potentially defamatory. Care should be taken to assert as a fact, only that which in the last analysis can be proved to be true. In many cases it will be sufficient to assert that allegations have been made to the local authority that the person has been violent, and that these cause the professionals concern for the children's safety. The social workers should take advice from the legal department if necessary. We do not think that the fear of proceedings ought to inhibit the social workers from taking necessary steps to protect the child.'

The inquiry thinks 'there should perhaps be more of a bias towards disclosure than there is at present'. (LJ 4.14-15)

Inquiries do not consider the effects on issues of confidentiality of parent or child attendance at case conferences or client access to records.

Accountability

Professional accountability, is formalised by accurately recording information. 'We have remarked on the way in which (the social worker) came up with new and often significant information which cannot be found in her file notes. We think this matters. Procedurally it meant that if anybody had to deputise for her they would be under-informed about things which turn out to be important. Substantially it meant that she maintained a personal hold on the case, because she had had it in her power to use or withhold information . . . it helped her skew the case conference appraisals.' (TH 4.30) 'Whatever the commitment to consistent noting of every facet of work in the management of the child abuse system, there is the overriding requirement that not merely should the social work always have a clear purpose, but also that the recording should be purposive so that readers of the information can immediately appreciate what was intended by the social worker in relation to each event.' (JB 224)

Record keeping

Good recording is an essential basis for good communication. While no substitute for clarity of purpose, high standards of practice and effective oral communication, good record keeping is a pre-requisite of all of these. The reports demonstrate problems in recording for all the agencies.

The purposes of careful, systematic contemporaneous recording are well summarised in the Shirley Woodcock inquiry: 'It shows many features of the case and action taken by the social worker. It provides advice on the history of the case and therefore can be used as a planning tool. It serves as a reference point for other social workers who have to take action in the absence of the social worker responsible for the case. It records important things in the life of the child which . . . may be necessary to explain to the child at a later date. It provides the basis of evidence for court proceedings. It provides a record for the department concerning performance of the statutory functions and the execution of its agreed policy. It provides basic studying for any inquiry which may be set up'. (SW 6.2)

Records should be complete. There are many examples of incompleteness of records (JB 228 for example). A file should contain key documents (SW 6.5) and should contain all relevant information known to the worker. The Lucy Gates Chairman's Report notes in relation to confidentiality, 'two growing tendencies: the first is to restrict the amount of information recorded and to record it in cryptic terms or in code form; the second is for professional workers to keep official records and also secret notes for their own and their colleagues information'. The inquiry considers that a failure to build up a full case file cannot be attributed to the refusal on the part of any other agency to make relevant information available. (LGC 66.2)

An incomplete record of events known to the worker can leave the worker vulnerable later: 'the letters to Linda Gates dated 1st December 1976 social worker 2 referred to the alleged injury. She told us in evidence that she must have been satisfied by Linda's explanation, otherwise she would have made a note on the case file'. (LGC 10.4) Lack of completeness can follow the practice of preparing poor case records in resumé) form. 'All social workers report must be in detail, prepared regularly as contact with the client or family is made or other events occur ... there is additional merit in adding the periodic summary.' (RF 64)

Accurate recording

In the Richard Fraser case it was not possible to determine with accuracy how regularly the social worker visited the family. (RF 64) It was not possible in the Beckford case to judge whether or not Jasmine had in fact been seen. The inquiry refers to health visitor recording or information would be recorded on the child's card even though he or she had not actually been seen but where somewhere had supplied the information. The inquiry emphasises the need for all sources of information and messages being made absolutely clear in the case record. (JB 227.229)

Inquiries refer to the need to ensure that significant incidents related to child abuse are fully documented. The practice of noting dates and times is commended. (LGP 6.15) An unpublished report makes the point that each child abuse file should contain a section outlining the details of the original incident, medical information, explanations, photographs etc. Over time, the perception of the original incident fails. This is especially so as staff change. Recording needs to be internally consistent (JB 227), factually accurate (SW 6.2 for example) and legible. (LGC 49)

Clarity

Records should be continuous and clear. (EJH 6.2) Good recording can shape the view of the case and stimulate further action 'Independently all the observations (about injuries and concerns) must have seemed insignificant. Together, in a well recorded file and with an understanding of the children and their circumstances, they would at least have warranted further investigation'. (SW 9.22)

Availability

Inquiries express concern about integrity of information systems in education, health and Social Services, to enable information held within the agency about the individual child to be integrated, and to bring together files about members of the same family.

School records

The Beckford inquiry notes the lack of any centralised system of recording information about child abuse registration or statutory orders in schools and says that 'it is necessary that each and every piece of personal information should find its way onto education index cards'. (JB 233) The Gates Panel were surprised at the absence of adequate records in schools, also. It recognised that the maintenance of school based records where sensitive and confidential family information is held is a problem for education, health and Social Services but the evidence suggests that a special system is necessary in relation to children who are suspected of being abused. (LGP 5.20)

The report goes on 'there is an obvious hiatus when a child starts school, and a question clearly does arise how much information during the pre-school years should be passed on. We think it must depend upon whether or not the child is still regarded as vulnerable by the time he starts school. Where that is the case, one would suspect that NAI to be recorded. More difficult is the child who has a number of 'accidents' where the explanation is accepted each time – just. We think it is probably possible to summarise those sort of concerns in a report to the school'. (LJ 6.7) 'Concern is sometimes expressed about labelling children in this way. One answer would be for there to be periodic reviews of such school health records. Another is that there should be a fresh record when a child transfers to secondary school, with only matters of continuing concern entered into it.' (LJ 6.8)

Community health records

In the Gates case it was noted that community health records and health visitors records were split between the surgeries with any general practice with which they happened to be attached and the child health concerns which they served. Hospital records kept at each hospital were voluminous . . . and had at times been moved between hospitals. (LGC 32) The problem in the health service essentially is how to get relevant information to professionals who need it at the right time. The Liam Johnson inquiry highlights problems which arise over the central filing of medical records on abused children within the health service. 'The effect of this, for example was that a doctor called on to examine and treat an injured child for which an accidental explanation was given, would have had no way of knowing that the same child or his sister had suffered a similar injury a year earlier and given a similar explanation. It seems to us obvious that such reports should form part of the medical file on the child.' (LJ 6.6)

Accessibility of health information

The accessibility of information in the health service is a recurrent theme. The Lucy Gates Chairman's Report notes that files were not always available in the Accident and Emergency Department where the child would be seen. Consideration should be given to the practice of providing an updated summary which should be fixed in the inner aspect of hospital case files so that instant key information could be available to any doctor who is asked to see the child, regardless of the presenting symptoms and signs. (LGC 56.1 and LGP 5.32) The Reuben Carthy inquiry is concerned that files are removed at the end of December in the A & E Department for the year of admission. The history of injuries can be an important feature in diagnosing and presenting injury and the inquiry recommends that the 'hospital should ensure that staff of the A & E Department have available the complete history of the knowledge of the child'.
(RC 58)

The Doreen Aston inquiry notes that 'Records were maintained in three separate documents: maternal and child health, which is a family record, the child record and the medical record used for clinic attendances. We found reference to three sets of records confusing; at times they duplicated and occasionally the same events were recorded in different terms. We recognise that this is a national problem but we consider that authorities should examine whether improvements could be made to their records system'. (DA 4.36)

Social Services records

Social Services are described as failing to bring together the files in relation to individual family members (for example LGC 23.3 and TH 4.1). Effective systems of central indexing are required, particularly in decentralised departments, 'Neither Sheffield nor Islington any longer operated a system whereby an index is maintained on all families and individuals who are known to the Social Services Department. In Islington, each neighbourhood office keeps its own index . . . Sheffield has a similar system, compounded in their case by the fact that the case is known only by the name of the person who first makes contact ... We do not consider that the only centralised index which does exist, namely the Child Protection Register, is sufficient. People do move within the borough, and do not always disclose previous involvement with Social Services'. (LJ 6.9-10)

Departmental reorganisations can affect the integrity of data. For example following the establishment of Social Services in 1971 the Gates inquiry was told that it would be several years before files of all persons or families known to this department were fully integrated. (LGC 23.3)

Inquiries also refer to the need for effective administration to facilitate retrieval of key information and juxtaposition of similar information, in a consistent 'house style'. ('A' 11 also SW 6.2, HK 3.20)

Security of records

The 'A' inquiry expresses concern about file security. Data must not be removed from files or destroyed ('A' 11), and files not lost (LGC 4.9, and EJH 2.1.9 for example).

Accessibility of records

Records should be accessible to professional workers who need them. This is particularly so in relation to staff providing cover whilst colleagues are on leave or sick. One aspect of access, in this context, is the need for prompt recording. Promptness is also necessary in relation to the evidential uses to which records may be put (for example CLV 8.9.35). A theme running through inquiries about the use of records is that while they may provide an important tool for the worker managing the case, they are as much, for the use of others (CLV 8.9.35 for example). The usefulness of one workers record keeping is diminished if information is not passed on to another who has an interest in receiving it. (LGC 57.7)

Records should be read

The records once written should be read. There are examples files not been read so that important information contained therein is missed. (TH 4.19, LGC 38.22 and DA 2.51)

Records and personal contact

Good record keeping and effective personal contact between professionals should run together. In the Beckford case 'each worker (social worker and health visitor) went her own way and their respective records were never cross referenced or inspected by the other'. The inquiry recommends that 'periodically – preferably as and when the two agencies representatives meet at case conferences or statutory case reviews – their records should be available to all those participants at those meetings for them to consult. If only the two workers on this case had compared notes, they would have quickly discovered that they were being told different and contradictory stories by Beverly Lorrington'. (JB 226) Such contact would also have overcome difficulties identified in the Aston inquiry over discrepant recording between health visitor and social worker. It refers to 'a number of discrepancies in recording which cumulatively emphasise the importance of workers ensuring that records are maintained accurately. This should include details of conversations where information is transmitted between workers'. (DA 2.64-65)

Transfer of cases

Face to face contact between professionals is particularly important at the point of transfer of the case, not least because inquiries repeatedly identify instances of delay in, or failure to transfer records either when workers change within agencies, or when families move. Personal contact at the time of handover opens a dialogue between professionals and is a link between the child's past and present experience.

Transfer of health records

The Carlile inquiry describes failures of transfer of medical records. Because medical records were not transferred, 'X was examined in a vacuum – no previous medical records, no knowledge of his immaturity, attention-seeking behaviour and tendency to fantasise, of his inclusion in the nurture group, of the possible child abuse allegation, or of the fact that he was being monitored'. (KC 168)

The inquiry notes problems about the division of health records between pre-school and school health which compounded problems of transfer of medical records into the authority from the Wirral. 'The records received in Greenwich in February 1986 came to the school health division, and did not percolate through to the pre-school health section. The senior medical officer responsible for the children aged 0–5 . . . did not even know of Kimberley's existence until after 8th June 1986 (when she died).' The records came to the senior medical officer (school health) except that she did not see all the records. She wrote a note asking for Kimberley to be medically examined at school but 'The trouble was that Kimberley was below school age and not attending the nursery. She was, therefore not available . . . for medical examination'. '(The) failure to promote further inquiries and to alert (the senior medical officer for pre school health) was the kind of error that was ultimately the product of a defective system. Records are records. There is no place in any information system for sifting out and separating the component parts of a unitary organisation's documentation. Records on all the children of the family should pass through one system, irrespective of the service appropriate to each one of the children.' (KC 124-126)

The Doreen Aston inquiry identifies that health visiting records took eighteen days to move between adjacent authorities. 'We are not the first to note problems of transfer of health visiting records. We believe that this is a matter to which the health authority should give urgent attention.' On this occasion one consequence was that the Southwark health visitor did not have the opportunity to discuss with the nurse manager who had been involved with the case from the beginning. 'The implications of her visit on the 9th July and her planning the context of the detailed background which she had now acquired.' (DA 2.199)

Transfer of information between Social Services

Transfer of information between authorities is a problem for Social Services too. In the Carlile case important discussions took place between the local team manager, working with the family, and the court welfare officer on the basis of her presumption that the Wirral had passed on all its extensive information about the Carlile family to Greenwich. It had not. (KC 114) The Liam Johnson inquiry considers that the way in which information is transferred between Social Services Departments might be improved. The transfer of whole case files being unwieldy and unworkable, it is essential that there should be a good summary of the known information when the case is transferred. (LJ 6.3) It recommends that 'central Government should consider problems of transfer of agency records further, the guidance in paragraph 5.6 of 'Working Together' being of very little help'. (LJ 8.18)

CONCLUSION

The purpose of this report was to identify key lessons to be learned from the child abuse inquiries of the 80s. The approach to this task was to read all the published inquiries, and a further eight unpublished reports – either Social Services Department Internal Reviews or Area Review Committee/Area Child Protection Committee Panel Reviews. Themes and issues have been collated in a way to allow relatively easy comparison with the previous DHSS analysis of inquiry reports 1973–81. I have added my own comments both for emphasis and where I think key points made by the inquiries have stood the test of the decade, and remain to be taken forward.

The impact of reading the inquiries en bloc and by chronological date of publication is very considerable.

The stories of the individual children are moving and the tragedy of the death, usually described near the middle of the report, is always moving impact. Afterwards, reading the policy and practice discussion seems rather superfluous. What really can be done? In the end, after the policy points have been taken on board or left as too case-specific, the stories of the children remain. Too few case studies of abused children are in the public domain and the inquiries are worth reading in full for them.

The limits of the inquiries

The task of this report – identifying key lessons to be learned – rather assumes that they have not been learned. There is no way of knowing. There is no mechanism by which practice is monitored nationally nor even a medium within which good case practice is routinely encouraged to be brought forward and published.

The inquiries vary in length from 20 to 300 pages and make from 4 to 90 recommendations. They take differing views about the breadth of their remit, and clearly find it difficult to generalise from an individual case about how services and organisations should operate. Generalising from 'failure' is self-evidently unsound. Moveover, the information available to the inquiry is partial. In a number of inquiries key players in the inter-agency network were not prepared to give evidence.

Other limitations are more profound. The inquiries focus on child abuse as a product of family interaction, and focus on members of the family as recipients of services following a point of referral. The effects of this are to exclude an analysis of child abuse within social structure, class, race and gender. The effects of environmental disadvantage are not generally analysed, and when referred to are with difficulty, if at all, tied into what happened. Secondly analysing families as recipients of services excludes what services might have helped prevent the abuse if they had been made available. Thirdly an analysis of what happened to the family as *people* rather than recipients of services is not found. The quest for understanding about why children are killed by some people and not others is scarcely taken forward. What models of child abuse can integrate social deprivation and individual pathology? How do we understand the family as a forum for child abuse? How do we interpret what we he, particularly from children?

A further limitation is to be found in the form which inquiries take – geared up to an adversarial process overseen by lawyers. The inquiries reflect upon themselves at considerable length – discussing the benefits of being held in private or public, the most effective manner of taking evidence, and the nature of their accountability. A theme running through this analysis of themselves in concern about delays in starting, concern about information being made available to it, and concern about how to obtain the attendance of key people. The resulting is something of a view of what happened, and who was to blame – rather than why.

It might reasonably be argued, in defence of inquiries, that they cannot be expected to analyse everything about child abuse -they cannot adopt that breadth of remit, and they are not primarily training or research, or even practice development aids. They are about the delivery of local services to a family in which a child abuse death occurred. In these terms, a key issue needs to be addressed further. That is the relationship between policies, procedures and practices of individual agencies in relation to child protection how these relate to the law, in particular to the statutory duties of the local authority and the most effective way in which the agencies can work together.

The inquiries in context

It does seem as though the child abuse inquiries have a life and history of their own. Writers in the field of social policy have variously identified the unintended and negative consequences of the child abuse inquiry, in particular the way in which they define child abuse in terms of individual pathology, how they stand to emphasise the role of the caring professions as 'social policing', and how they serve to give the community a feeling of doing something in a climate or moral panic. Two points have struck most forcibly.

Firstly, the fragmentation – isolation – of child protection services from the rest of child care. The inquiries are only the most extreme form of special arrangements – legal and administrative, for scrutinising for child protection services as distinct from the rest of the services which children in need should receive. This is not just an academic or ideological point. Its practical application, for example in the way professions advise and assist the local authority, and meet together in a case conference or case review context – directly affects services received by the child and family.

Secondly, the inquiries represent in an extreme form the polarisation of points of view, and of people, in a framework that is supposed to bring people into working together. This is not just reflected in the adversarial nature of the inquiries but also in the stance of the media to these major public events, and in the polarisation of the children's interests versus the parents interests versus public interests versus professional interests.

On the assumption that when a child dies following abuse it is reasonable for local services to consider whether services should have been provided that were not, or when they were were provided inadequately, a different approach to child abuse inquiries is needed. The inquiries of the 80s have all, with the exception of the Cleveland inquiry, been commissioned by local agencies or the ACPC. Yet the Lucy Gates inquiry at the beginning of the decade, and the Liam Johnson inquiry at the end were expressing concern about the adequacy of Government guidelines for this process. The role of the ACPC should be emphasised in this respect. Revised guidelines are needed to encompass the conduct of reviews by individual agencies, their collation in a reasonable time scale by the ACPC, and a framework for the conduct of inter-agency inquiries by the ACPC itself. This revision could usefully place a priority on the attendance of key professional personnel, and how to take evidence from the public, parents and children. Further guidelines are needed for inquiries into cases of extreme public concern when an independent panel is called into an area to inquire into case management. Particular attention should be given to guidance around the remit of such an inquiry. It is clear that independent panels have felt daunted by their task when asked to comment not only on the child protection aspects of the case but also 'lessons to be learned' for the whole of their commissioning organisations.

A trend has emerged towards the end of the 80s in which the Social Services Inspectorate carries out a parallel inquiry into child protection services, whilst the case inquiry is proceeding, or before and after it. This trend needs careful management. Whilst an attempt to broaden an inquiry into an investigation of services may be desirable, an artificial boundary between child protection services and services to children in need, or in care, can be imposed. There needs to be a clear set of standards regulating inquiries, these inspections, and every day practice.

The inquiries struggle both with defining their standards of judgement – usually 'what could reasonably be expected on the basis of what was known at the time' – and defining standards of professional practice. The SSI reviews have adopted standards taken from 'Working Together' and more recently other Government documents. What is needed is an integrated standard of practice for child protection, integrating it with child care, and capably of being continuously monitored by local agencies for the purpose the improvement of local services, and by central Government for the purposes of bridging the gap between practice and policy.

Thereafter, individual agencies should establish their standards of practice before they can effectively engage in inter-agency working. Child protection must be seen as a priority by all the relevant agencies in order for effective inter-agency working to take place. As importantly, each agency must consider its duties to protect in the context of its duties to care. Only then can effective inter-agency working be embarked upon. Inter-agency working is not self evidently useful. It certainly is not easy and must be energetically and strategically pursued. An ACPC plan is needed which reflects joint planning strategies in each local authority and health area.

The same kind of integration is needed in respect of training at both a national and local level. The inquiries make a number of interesting comments about training and yet the reader is left with no clear view about what kind of training is most needed. Local and national training strategies are surely needed which avoid both duplication, and reinventing the wheel, and allow best training practice to be established.

The Department Of Health, rightly eager to implement the Cleveland findings has created it seems in its 'Working Together' document a considerable gap between policy and practice. The gap needs to be bridged.

The most important single outcome from inquiries of the 80s has been the establishment of a set of principles for professional relationships to parents and children, in the Cleveland report. Yet if this to be more than a convention of good manners strategies for turning policy into practice and sharing best practice, nationally, need to be developed. Lessons are to be learned elsewhere than the child abuse inquiries: the funding of research; the promulgation of information – both about individual inquiries and developing practice; and most importantly the way in which organisations 'learn' about themselves and monitor performance and improve standards of practice.

There is a view that child care and child protection are solely – at best mainly – the prerogative of the welfare agencies. Of course this is not so. It is parents who kill their children, not professional agencies. Yet it is a reflection on the fragmentation of the care of children within our society that welfare agencies are howlingly blamed when 'things go wrong'. The public is ambivalent about what it wants from services – in particular how intrusive into families professional workers should be, and how much services should cost. At the same time we are ambivalent about child abuse and child protection – what is proper care, what is reasonably chastisement, what is the sexual component of 'normal' family interaction, how do we understand the family?

Professionals, the public, parents and children themselves must work together to protect children and prevent child abuse. 'The child is a person and not an object of concern' has become the motto for child protection services in the late 80s. How this is put into effect by professionals, the public, parents and children to inform the delivery of services case by case, is the key question for preventing child abuse and protecting children in the 90s.

appendices

This list includes inquiries published in 1980 and 1981 not included in the previous summary of inquiries.

The Number in brackets denotes order of publication.

Secretary of State Inquiry

Report of the Inquiry into Child Abuse in Cleveland 1987 (15)
Secretary of State for Social Services
Published July 1988

Local Inquiries

Mr and Mrs 'A' (19)
Humberside Child Protection Committee
Summary report published

Doreen ASTON (17)
Lambeth, Lewisham and Southwark Area Review Committee
Published July 1989

Jasmine BECKFORD (9)
London Borough of Brent and Brent Health Authority
Published December 1985

Jason CAESAR (4)
Cambridgeshire Social Services Committee
Published February 1982

Kimberley CARLILE (14)
London Borough of Greenwich and Greenwich Health Authority
Published December 1987

Reuben CARTHY (8)
Nottinghamshire Area Review Committee
Standing Inquiry Panel
Published September 1985

Richard FRASER (5)
London Borough of Lambeth, Inner London Education Authority,
Lambeth Southwark and Lewisham Area Health Authority (Teaching)
Published May 1982

Lucy GATES (6)
London Borough of Bexley and Greenwich and Bexley Health
Authority
Published July 1982
   1 Chairman's Report
   2 Report of other Panel Members

Claire HADDON (1)
City of Birmingham Social Services Department
Published February 1980

Tyra HENRY (12)
London Borough of Lambeth
Published 1987

Emma Jane HUGHES (3)
Borough Council of Calderdale
Published November 1981

Liam JOHNSON (18)
Islington Area Child Protection Committee
Published November 1989

Heidi KOSEDA (10)
Hillingdon Area Review Committee
Published March 1986

Karl John McGOLDRICK (16)
Northern Regional Health Authority
Published June 1989

Christopher PINDER/Daniel FRANKLAND (2)
Bradford Area Review Committee – Child Abuse
Published July 1981

Jason PLISCHKOWSKY (13)
Hampshire County Council
Published February 1988

Charlene SALT (11)
Oldham District Review Committee
Published October 1986

Shirley WOODCOCK (7)
London Borough of Hammersmith and Fulham
Summary report published August 1984

	CLV	'A'	DA	JB	JC	KC	RC	RF	LG	CH	TH	EJH	LJ	HK	KMcG	CP	JP	CS	SW
Workers & others involved																			
Social Worker	X	X	X	X	X	X	X	X	X	X	X	X	X	X	X	X	X	X	X
Police	X	X	X					X	X		X		X	X	X		X		
Police Surgeon	X													X					
NSPCC	X								X					X					
Child Abuse Consultant Co-ordinator					X	X			X					X					
GP	X	X		X	X	X	X		X				X		X	X	X		X
Health Visitor		X	X	X	X	X	X	X	X	X	X		X	X	X	X	X	X	X
Paediatrician	X	X		X	X			X	X						X				X
Psychiatrist	X								X										
Accident & Emergency Dept				X	X		X	X	X				X		X		X	X	X
Nurse	X		X		X									X				X	
School Nurse						X		X											
Midwife			X					X		X				X				X	
Day Nursery Staff			X	X	X			X	X									X	X
Teacher		X		X		X		X	X	X			X						
Childminder								X											
Education Welfare Officer/ Social Worker	X			X			X	X	X	X				X					
Psychologist	X	X						X											
Probation Officer								X			X		X					X	
Housing Welfare Officer											X								
Homeless Persons Officer/ Unit											X		X						X
Social Security Officer								X											
Home Help/Family Aide								X									X		
Independent S.W./Guardian			X												X	X	X		
Court Welfare Officer						X													
Magistrate	X			X														X	
Family	X		X				X				X			X	X				
Foster Parents	X	X		X		X			X			X		X		X	X		
Neighbours									X					X	X				

Printed in the United Kingdom for HMSO.
Dd.0293814, 4/91, C75, 3385/4, 5673, 144773.